FIRE-UP Your Presentations & FIRE-UP Your Results

What others are saying about "FIRE-UP"

"FIRE-UP Your Presentations and FIRE-UP Your Results is an easy and informative read that takes you on a journey through the how-to's of effectively structuring and delivering a compelling presentation."

–Anthony Robbins
Author, *Awaken the Giant Within* and *Unlimited Power*

"Tom McCarthy's *FIRE-UP Your Presentations & FIRE-UP Your Results* book will help executives and managers move their teams to action and it will help salespeople shorten the sales cycle and close more sales. If you are an executive, a manager or a salesperson, this book is a must read."

–Brian Tracy
Chairman & CEO, Brian Tracy Learning Systems

"Working with Tom and reading his book has helped me be better prepared for professional and personal growth! Tom's tremendous contribution has made a difference in my effectiveness as a leader in implementing change. In a large company we all work extremely hard to build a stronger company and team. The FIRE-UP book gives us tools that helps us accomplish our goals."

–Dawn Maroney
Vice President, PacifiCare

"FIRE-UP Your Presentations & FIRE-UP Your Results is the best book written on designing and delivering persuasive presentations. Tom's system is powerful and it works! Every organization that has managers or salespeople giving persuasive presentations needs to learn and use the FIRE-UP System."

–Gino Blefari
Chairman and CEO, Intero Real Estate

"Tom's "Fire -Up" system of persuasive presentations is perfect for anybusiness leader whose responsibilities include public speaking. The simple format is practical and powerful. After reading Tom's book and applying his principles anyone can improve their communication skills. I am absolutely convinced that he has written one of the most effective books of it's kind. Well done!"

–**Troy McQuagge**
President, UGA Insurance

"The *FIRE-UP Your Presentations & FIRE-UP Your Results* is a must read for anyone who wants to be a better communicator. Whether beginner or seasoned pro, Tom McCarthy tells you how to do it with simplicity. The practical strategies make FIRE-UP a real treasure on every leaders' bookshelf. After reading FIRE-UP, I literally can't wait to give my next speech or presentation and use the lessons I've learned!"

–**T.D. Decker**
Former CEO of Telemotive and Shaped Wire

"Tom McCarthy is an outstanding presenter and coach and his *FIRE-UP Your Presentations & FIRE-UP Your Results* is an absolute must for anyone who wants to take their presentation skills to the highest level! Tom has an amazing ability to connect with any audience and take them on an emotional journey with him. This book will help you identify the true outcome you are looking for in any presentation and provide you with the strategy and tools to achieve that outcome."

–**David Healy**
Managing Director, Scottish Equitable International

"The straightforward technique boosted the skills of both engineers and sales people in the class, and has remained a guiding concept to assist class participants out in the field. The results achieved are excellent, apply broadly to different people and have given lasting value. The instructor, technique and results are awesome!"

–Jim Niblack
Manager of Channel Operations, Cisco Systems

"Communicating and presenting innovation in advance technology is critical for my team's success. Tom's FIRE-UP training is a mandatory requirement for sales and consulting engineering people joining my team. My team is composed of the 'best of the best', they utilize the techniques learned in Tom's course to deliver the Cisco message to truly impact our sales. I truly believe Tom's material has helped us meet and surpass our sales goals as an organization.
"Tom's material is incredibly empowering for my team, he weaves a message to 'Play Full Out' into his course which aligns very well with our organizational goals (stretch mentality)."

–Paul Werner
Regional Manager, Cisco Systems

"With this book,Tom McCarthy has uniquely leveraged his lifetime study of Presentation Mastery into an insightful, clear and compelling system.A remarkable book!"

–Richard Davies
General Manager, Coca-Cola Enterprises Ltd.

Tom McCarthy

FIRE-UP Your Presentations
& FIRE-UP Your Results

─────────○─────────

**A Powerful System for Creating and
Delivering Outstanding Presentations**

Copyright © MMIV by Tom McCarthy

For more information about Tom McCarthy visit
www.TomMcCarthy.com or www.FireUpTraining.com

Publisher's Cataloging-in-Publication Data

McCarthy, Tom, 1961-
  Fire-up your presentations & fire-up your results/
  [Tom McCarthy].-- 1st ed.
  p. cm.
  LCCN 2003114654
  ISBN 0974436313
  1. Business presentations. 2. Public speaking.
I. Title.

HF5718.22.M33 2003   658.4'52
                         QBI03-200941

Dedication

First and foremost I dedicate this book to my mother Lucille Berenice McCarthy, who passed away in October of 2002. She was a leader who dedicated herself to her children, raising my two brothers and I on her own after my father's death. My mother taught me the importance of integrity and putting others first, which is integral in the FIRE-UP System and in any meaningful communication.

Another early influence on me was my grandfather. I used to love to listen to him tell his stories of World War II and his encounters and friendships with people like Winston Churchill and Dwight Eisenhower. I could listen to him for hours.

Lt. Gen. Hank Emerson, a dear friend to my father and my mother as well as my brothers and I, was another role model as a communicator. He could motivate a group of troops to take on any challenge. He loved his soldiers and it showed. They would follow him anywhere.

Dr. Paul Brandes, my pre law speech teacher at the University of North Carolina sparked my interest in speaking and training as a career. He saw something in me that I did not see in myself and he asked me to be a teaching assistant for his class. It was my first opportunity to help others to improve their communication skills and I am forever grateful to him.

Tony Robbins showed me what was possible as a communicator. He challenged the norms of speaking and created a whole new captivating way of conducting trainings. Anyone who has seen him speak leaves in awe of the way he combines education with empowerment and entertainment. He is one of a kind.

Brandy Weld gave me the first opportunity to work with Cisco Systems when she invited me to speak at the FAST courses Cisco delivers to all new team members.

Kate Dow, Patrick Wallace, Jim Dajani, Gordon Jendraziak, Shawn Kieft, Jen Murray, Maryann Slee, Omar Sultan, Cheryl Sultan and Mary Beth Rogers have given me the opportunity to continue to develop the FIRE-UP System by entrusting me to teach FIRE-UP to hundreds of Cisco team members each year. Their trust and belief in me is something I treasure and it continues to drive me to improve.

Vicky St. George worked her magic in taking my concepts and stories and making them work together in this book. I am lucky to know her and it has been an honor working with her. When Vicky was finished the book became Ford Saeks project. He took the manuscript and turned it into the book you are holding in your hands. Ford and Cyndy Bressler have helped me with many projects over the years and I am thankful to have them as part of my team.

Last but not least I want to thank my wife Stacy and my two children Kylie and Tommy. They provide a solid base of support and love from which I can create. They inspire me with their zest for life and their concern for making the world a better place. I love them with all my heart.

–Tom McCarthy

Table of Contents

Introduction .... *i*

Chapter One
No One's a Born Speaker 1
Great Speakers Create a Series of Interesting,
    Connected Conversations 3
It's Not About You! 5
The Four Major Outcomes of the FIRE-UP System 7
Chapter 1 Highlights 10

Chapter Two
What is a Powerful and Persuasive Presentation? 11
The Four Levels of Presentations 14
Chapter 2 Highlights 18

Chapter Three
Climbing the Ladder of Outstanding Presentations 19
Chapter 3 Highlights 22

Chapter Four
Know Where Your Ladder Leads 23
What Does Your Audience Want and Need? 25
Make Sure You're the Right Person for the Job 28
The Seven Characteristics of a Powerful Outcome 29
Chapter 4 Highlights 35

Chapter Five
Create a Rock Solid Foundation 37
Get to Know Your Audience 37
Chapter 5 Highlights 44

Chapter Six
Prepare Yourself-Phase Two 46
Your OPI Emotional Recipe 47
Accessing your OPI Emotions 51
The Physiology of Confidence 55
Getting Rid of Disempowering Patterns of Physiology,
    Language, and Beliefs 80
Chapter 6 Highlights 87

Chapter Seven
Presentation Day 89
Meeting Your Audience 98
Chapter 7 Highlights 101

Chapter Eight
Communicate With Integrity and Power 103
Chapter 8 Highlights 107

Chapter Nine
FIRE 'EM UP! 109

Chapter Ten
F=Focus Your Audience's Attention 111
Secret #1 113
Secret #2 114
Secret #3 116
Secret #4 120
Chapter 10 Highlights 124

Chapter Eleven
I=Inform Your Audience of Your Purpose 125
Chapter 11 Highlights 132

Chapter Twelve
R=Remind Your Audience of Their Pain 133
Chapter 12 Highlights 143

Chapter Thirteen
E=Educate, Empower, and Entertain Your Audience 145
Chapter 13 Highlights 157

Chapter Fourteen
U=Use Your Audience's Uniqueness to Demonstrate a
    Solution to Their Problems 159
Chapter 14 Highlights 165

Chapter Fifteen
P=Propose a Commitment Close With Connection 167
Five Steps to an Effective Close 171
Chapter 15 Highlights 177

Chapter Sixteen
Secrets of the World's Top Speakers 179
How to Become a World Class Presenter 189
Chapter 16 Highlights 193

Chapter Seventeen
Conclusion: Climbing the Real Ladder of Success 195

Recommended Resources *199*

Introduction
Why You Need This Book

"Joe, I need you to present this project at the company's next Board of Directors meeting . . ."

"Sally, we're counting on you to close $1,000,000 worth of business with your customer presentations next week. And we really need this business if we're going to hit our numbers . . ."

"Congratulations, Pete! Your team is getting an award for outstanding performance. The company's throwing a banquet, and they've invited you to give the acceptance speech . . ."

"Mom, my school is having a Career Day next month. Can you come in and talk? It'd really mean a lot to me..."

Sound familiar? When you're asked to speak to a group, what's your response? An enthusiastic "yes"? An offhand "sure"? Or does the invitation cause your stomach to do jumping jacks and your knees to get a little weak? If so, you're not alone. Year after year when people are asked about their greatest fear, public speaking tops the list Why is this true? Most of us have no trouble talking one-on-one. What is it about standing up in front of a group that turns us from accomplished communicators into tongue-tied amateurs? More important, how can we become clear, passionate, persuasive speakers who can move people to take action?

I've been a student of persuasive communication ever since taking a pre-law speech course at the University of North Carolina, Chapel Hill, in 1981. My teacher, Dr. Paul Brandes, was a master at helping students develop a love for persuasive speaking. After completing the class, I was asked to serve as a teaching assistant for Dr. Brandes, and my passion for helping others become persuasive speakers began.

My first job out of college, as a stockbroker for a regional investment firm, offered a few chances to develop my speaking skills. I taught a class at the local community college on investing for novices and because of my success as a young broker I was asked to help train other new brokers who were joining the firm.

But it was in 1987 when I joined Robbins Research International, a training and development firm headed by Anthony Robbins, that my development as a speaker and a trainer of other speakers became a full-time occupation. I was hired as a regional sales manager to lead a team that was marketing business seminars for Anthony Robbins. I started out in Dallas, Texas, with a bunch of other young, "hot shot" salespeople who were just as eager as I was to succeed. We would go to companies and do presentations in front of sales teams, management teams, customer service teams, and so on. But while we had a great product and some clear ideas about persuading the customer, we didn't get a lot of training on speaking in front of groups.

Now, many of us did well simply because we were passionate about our product. But I was the head of the sales team, and that meant I was responsible for training all of the new sales reps. I not only had to do a great job of selling seminars myself, but I also had to teach others to do persuasive presentations as well.

I observed great speakers whenever possible. I studied how other salespeople worked in front of groups. I dissected my own performance after every single presentation, evaluating what worked and what didn't, making changes and then evaluating the results. I taught what I was learning to my sales team and coached them through their first, second, tenth, and twentieth presentations. I noticed what was happening when speakers were struggling. More important, I observed speakers when they were in the "zone" where they really connected with the audience and speaking became effortless. And every time I found myself in that "zone," I would do everything I could to capture exactly what I had done to get and keep myself there.

The success and closing rates of my sales team rose so high that I became the company's national sales manager. Later, when I started my own training and development company and began speaking to audiences all over the world, I found that after almost every presentation someone would come up to me and say, "You're so persuasive and you seem to have such a great time when you speak. Would you be willing to coach me on speaking skills?" So I began coaching selected individuals using my FIRE-UP System of Persuasive Presentations, helping them to structure and deliver persuasive presentations that they loved to give and audiences loved to hear.

In 1999, I was hired to speak at and help facilitate Cisco Systems' (one of the leading technology companies in the world) new employee orientation program called FAST. The presentations I gave at FAST consistently received high ratings and the audience liked my speaking style. Within a few months I was asked to customize my FIRE-UP System for Cisco executives, managers, salespeople and engineers so that they could improve their ability to deliver persuasive presentations. My principal occupation is still delivering leadership and peak performance teambuilding training to audiences all over the world, but since offering my FIRE-UP classes through Cisco I have spent several days each year focused on training groups of professional business people to communicate positively and persuasively and enjoy themselves in the process.

This book will show you how to master the two most important elements of a persuasive presentation. First, you'll learn to structure your message effectively to take your audience from where they are to where you want them to end up. Remember, a presentation is only effective if it produces a pre-determined result that you intended it to achieve. Second, you'll discover how to deliver your message in such a way that your audience is moved emotionally so they will *want* to go with you to your ultimate goal. As Tony Robbins taught me a long time ago, a presentation is the transfer of emotion. You must get your audience to feel empowering feelings about the information and ideas that you are delivering.

This system for persuasive presentations can be applied in every area of your life where you want to persuade individuals or groups. Whether you're talking to your spouse about a ski trip, your kids about staying away from drugs, the parents of your Little League Team or the P.T.A. about a new ballfield, your city council about improvements to your community, your boss about a raise, your latest prospect about a million-dollar contract, your co-workers about an important project, your management team about a company reorganization, or an audience of thousands about a revolutionary idea or project, you must be able to communicate your ideas clearly in a way that will engage the emotions as well as logic. Equally important, you must *enjoy* the process of communicating. Your enjoyment and a relaxed approach will aid you in persuading others of your message, and will make presentations something you look forward to with excitement and anticipation instead of dread.

But for you to become a powerful communicator, you can't just read this book; you must use what it contains. There are four keys to gaining the most from this book.

1. Play full out. This book will teach you a complete system for consistently delivering outstanding presentations, but just reading the book will not make you a better presenter. To be a better presenter you must make a commitment now to master the FIRE-UP System and do the exercises in this book as if the future of you and your family depended on it. Your level of commitment will determine your level of success. Improvement as a persuasive speaker will only come if you consistently push through your current limitations. My best presentations always come when I use the FIRE-UP System and remind myself to "use everything!" When I hold back in any way my presentations always suffer. I challenge you to play full out in learning and implementing the FIRE-UP System. If you do, I promise that you will soon be able to give presentations that will captivate your audiences and move them to action.

2. Capture the information. I've created a simple system, FIRE-UP, which will lead you one step at a time to creating and delivering persuasive presentations. But you need to make sure you understand every step along the way and apply them in the order they're given. Don't skip from one step to the other, or leave out a step because it's harder than the rest. Follow the path laid out in this book and it will lead you to your goal of becoming a dynamic, powerful, persuasive communicator.

3. Have fun! What if you could have a blast every time you stood up in front of people to share your ideas? It starts by having a good time doing the exercises in this book. The more fun you start associating to presentations now, the more fun you'll have when you're actually in front of a group. Great presenters love being with their audiences. Even when the audiences are difficult customers, angry shareholders, or cranky team members, we can still choose to have fun engaging them in the process of moving to a better outcome. Later in the book we will share with you some ideas to make presenting more fun, but start right now by making a commitment to choose to make presentations something that you enjoy and look forward to.

4. Use what you learn. How many people do you know who have gotten a book on a diet, or bought one of those electric organizers, or put a new software program on their computer, and never used any of them? This system will not work through osmosis; to become a truly persuasive presenter you must take every opportunity to practice what you learn. Luckily, you can use the principles of this system with one person or a thousand. You can even practice in front of the family pet! But the old adage "Use it or lose it" applies doubly to presentation skills. I firmly believe that the FIRE-UP System has everything you need to be an outstanding presenter. But we are all creatures of habit. You have spent many years developing thoughts and habits relating to giving presentations. Some of these thoughts and habits are powerful and they will continue to assist you in being an outstanding presenter, but other thoughts and habits you have may be holding you back. For you to grow as a speaker, you must break through the old disempowering thoughts and habits and be willing to apply the new ones you'll learn through the FIRE-UP System. Use every opportunity to improve. Make what you learn a part of your regular one-on-one communication, and you'll find these skills will be at your fingertips when you stand in front of groups.

No matter whether you consider yourself a great presenter or the worst speaker on God's earth, the ideas in this book will help you get better. I have seen significant improvement in every person that I have ever worked with. I'd like to think it is all because of me, but the truth is you already have what it takes to be an outstanding presenter inside of you now. This book is designed to help you tap into that power to communicate persuasively that is already within you. All it will take is a little time, a little openness to learning and to trying new ways of doing things, and your commitment to mastering the FIRE-UP System. Let's begin!

Chapter One
No One's a Born Speaker —
But Speaking is Natural

Back in 1988, I was in Los Angeles, California, getting ready to speak in front of a thousand people at a sales training seminar. My job was to do a three-minute introduction for the main speaker of the day. I'd been the national sales manager for the training company for a couple of years, and I was pretty comfortable doing presentations before groups of five to fifty people. But a thousand? That was terrifying.

I had all kinds of things prepared, but when I went onstage I forgot everything I wanted to say. I was so nervous I babbled a few sentences and then, my voice cracking, said, "Please welcome Tony Robbins!" and ran offstage as fast as I could. It was embarrassing, humiliating, terrifying-all the adjectives most people associate with the words "public speaking." I was a total failure. Me, the guy who was supposed to be the best at persuading people! I vowed I would never let something like that happen to me again.

Today, I make my living as a speaker and consultant, offering seminars and training sessions all over the world. I'm not trying to say that I know everything about speaking, or that I've got it all handled when it comes to my own presentations-in fact, just the opposite. I'm fundamentally a shy person. Being a public speaker was never my goal growing up, and I think the same is true for most people. That's why I consider myself a walking, talking example of the fact that *anyone* can learn to be a persuasive communicator, whether the audience is five people or five thousand. And I have developed a clear, easy system that will show you step by step how to create and deliver persuasive presentations in any context, with ease and enjoyment.

I call it the "FIRE-UP" System because the letters F-I-R-E-U-P stand for different aspects of creating powerful and persuasive presentations. But I also like the term "fire up!" because that describes what every great presenter must do. When I look at an audience that I am about to address, the first thing I do is focus on the outcome or result that I will be creating through my presentation. If I have a powerful solution or outcome that will truly benefit these people, then I know that they have the potential to embrace my outcome. But just because they have the potential to embrace it does not mean that they necessarily will. *It is my job to make sure they do!* The audience's potential to embrace the outcome of my presentation is similar to a small flickering flame. If the flickering flame is not fed with the proper fuel, it will eventually be extinguished. My presentation is the fuel for that flame. If I deliver the necessary information in the proper pattern of persuasion and with the proper emotions, then I can FIRE-UP the flickering flame of potential in each audience member into a rip-roaring fire that drives them to embrace my outcome.

But in order to fire up the audience, the presenter also must be "fired up" as well. We've all sat through dreadful presentations by speakers who either hate what they're doing, or, what's almost worse, they're bored doing the same old speech yet again. To be persuasive, you must be excited about what you have to offer. Only when you are emotionally engaged *yourself* will you be able to move your audience as well. Whether it's your first speech or your five hundredth, you must be committed to your audience and emotionally involved in your content.

At this point you may be thinking, *I don't want to be a professional speaker, Tom-what will this book do for me?* Well, if you are going to be a leader in any organization, or if you are going to persuade a customer to embrace a new solution, you'd better be able to express yourself in a powerful way. One of the best examples I have seen of this is the CEO of Cisco Systems, John Chambers. Through the FAST program at Cisco I have had the opportunity to listen to John speak to new Cisco team members as they are educated about the Cisco culture. As excited as the audience is about being a part of Cisco when John starts his presentation, they are always even more excited and committed to Cisco when he is finished speaking. Though his communication he always moves his audience to a better and more productive place. They leave his presentations with even stronger beliefs about themselves and Cisco, and a resolve to deliver outstanding individual and team performance. It's no wonder that many people regard John as one of the world's top CEOs.

Truthfully, the ability to persuade groups is essential in today's business climate. More and more businesses are structured around teams, and everyone needs to be able to communicate comfortably and effectively within a team environment. The skills you will learn in these pages are applicable to almost every situation-not just presentations where you're standing up in front of a group, but at tables or board meetings or sales conferences or department meetings or the P.T.A. Indeed, these skills can be used *whenever* you communicate, whether it's with one person or a group.

Great Speakers Create a Series of Interesting, Connected Conversations

Speaking is one of the fundamental activities of the human race. In fact, it's one of the few things that separates us from other animals. Speaking is something we learn to do as babies and usually keep doing until we die. So what is it about speaking to groups that turns us from experienced talkers into terrified, tongue-tied amateurs? Standing up in front of a group of people seems to make us forget how to talk naturally. We start doing things that are not normal or natural: talking above people's heads, listening to our own inner dialogue instead of focusing on the audience, using stilted language or bad jokes-the kind of stuff we would never do when we're talking to one person. Being in front of an audience is scary. We feel exposed. We're afraid of looking like fools. But most of us think that because speaking makes us scared or uncomfortable that we'll never be any good at it. And nothing could be further from the truth.

I don't believe anyone is a "born" speaker-and I also believe that public speaking is a skill anyone can develop. To become a persuasive communicator, however, you need to realize that speaking in front of a group is no different than having a conversation with another person. In fact, that's all you're really doing. *An effective presentation is simply a series of interesting, connected conversations.* Viewed this way, speaking to a group becomes something very natural and normal. It's kind of like being at a party: you have one conversation, then move on to another person or group and have another conversation, and so on.

What do you do when you have a conversation with someone? You do your best to find something in common with them. You look at them directly. You smile at them and use your voice qualities and physiology to make what you say interesting. You ask them questions. You read their responses and change your communication as a result. You speak informally, casually, in a normal, conversational tone of voice. You use humor. You're not afraid to express yourself passionately on a subject. Now, think about the ways great presenters communicate. Don't they do exactly what I just described, only they do it with audiences? They're comfortable. They are genuinely interested in their audience. They try to find something in common with the people they're speaking to. They ask questions. They smile. They speak normally and naturally; they don't use elevated language that no one understands. They often use humor. They're not afraid of being passionate about their subject. And people often say after the presentation is done, "You know, I felt like s/he was speaking directly to me!" That's because most great presenters know that giving a speech is not that different from having a conversation. *You simply speak to one person at a time*, staying with each person long enough to create a connection and then moving on to the next person, while using all your communication skills to make the conversation interesting for your audience. The outcome is simple: to touch other human beings with thoughts, words, and emotions and move them to a pre-defined outcome.

It's Not About You!

There's another secret that great presenters know that makes it far easier to get up and speak. Here it is: *"The presentation is not about you! It is all about your audience!"* If you've ever felt nervous before a presentation, it's usually because you were focused on yourself, not on your audience. My advice to you is forget about yourself and put all your focus on how you can use your presentation to move your audience to an outcome that is better for them. When you are totally focused on serving others your nervousness will tend to melt away and you will deliver a presentation that will seem effortless. Remember, everyone is evaluating a presentation with one unconscious question: "What's in it for me?" And if you put your focus on your audience instead of yourself, you're 99 percent of the way to persuading and influencing them.

This goes against what most presenters tend to do when faced with an audience of strangers. Most of us feel a lot of pressure to "perform." We think the audience is judging us, and that we should do certain things (like use a loud voice or stilted gestures or formal language) and not do other things (like talk directly to one person in the audience). But if you've ever had a moment in front of a group-whether it's your family or your golf foursome or your Sunday school class—when you've been in the "flow" of a presentation, you'll realize that in that moment you're completely focused on the people in front of you. You don't worry what you look like or how you sound; you're completely committed to getting your point across to these individuals. And what happens in those moments is far more powerful than any prepared, scripted presentation could ever be.

Early in my speaking career I was asked to give a sales presentation for a real estate company in Los Angeles. I drove up from San Diego, and as I started getting close to the company's address, I noticed that I was going deeper and deeper into one of the worst sections of Los Angeles, where poverty and crime were rampant. I began having second thoughts about even doing this presentation, and those thoughts were strengthened when I saw the company office building. There were bars on all the windows, and a chain link fence topped with barbed wire surrounded the parking lot. I thought about turning my car around and just going home. After all, the people in this company probably wouldn't have any money to invest in seminars. And they probably weren't going to be interested in what I had to say anyway. I had almost turned my car around to go home when I realized I didn't want to speak to this audience because I was focused on myself. I was afraid of not being well received, of not being able to achieve my outcome. Once I realized this, I drove into the company's parking lot and changed my focus from myself to my audience. I thought about the impact I could have by helping each person in my audience see the greatness in themselves, and how I could help to create a ripple of hope in this area of despair. I made up my mind to deliver a presentation that was totally focused on helping the people in this company to achieve their goals and dreams. As soon as I made this commitment, all hesitation and nervousness faded away, to be replaced with passion, confidence, and a sincere caring for my audience. The result? A presentation where I knew I had done my best and an audience that didn't want me to leave.

In addition, everyone there also registered for the sales training program I was selling-not because I had some fabulous close but because I truly cared about them, and they saw how my product could improve their lives. That day I truly learned that every presentation is an opportunity to serve the audience, not yourself. And if you take great care of your audience and make them your priority, you will get everything you want for yourself and more. Realizing that speaking isn't about me but about my audience made me feel as if a weight was lifted off my back. I didn't have to impress anyone or make people think I was a great "presenter." Instead, my job was to care about the people in the audience, to share valuable information with them in a dynamic way that would move them emotionally and persuade them to take action. My focus shifted from, "How am I doing?" to "How are *they* doing?" And with that shift, my presentations improved exponentially.

Remember that your audience wants to know not how great you'll be but what you have to offer them. When you keep your focus on your audience instead of on yourself, and if you remember that your ultimate responsibility is simply to connect and converse with the people in your audience, you'll find your communication with groups will become easier, more pleasant, and far more effective.

The Four Major Outcomes of the FIRE-UP System

Later in this book we'll review all the components of the FIRE-UP System. But let's conclude this chapter by telling you exactly what you can expect to gain by reading this book and putting this system into practice.

You can expect to . . .

1. **Significantly improve your results as a persuasive presenter.**
   When I train speakers in the FIRE-UP System, I work only with a few people at a time, ten to seventeen at most. We videotape each speaker and work intensely on the "differences that make the difference": the small changes that will have the most impact on the quality of their presentations. I believe that by implementing even

a few of the skills and suggestions in this book, you will experience the same kind of night and day improvement that my students see in themselves.

2. **Add more value to your audiences.**
   If there were one belief, one idea that will make the biggest difference in your ability to persuade your audiences, it's the idea that *presentations are opportunities to add more value.* What can you show your audience that will make their lives easier, better, happier? How can you help them experience more good emotions? What can you say or do that will have a positive impact on their lives? When you add more value, invariably you will get more back in return-more emotional involvement, more agreement, more results.

   And that's value as your audience defines it, not the way you define it. You may think your product or idea is the greatest thing since sliced bread, but it if doesn't meet the needs of this particular group of people, your ability to persuade will be very limited. In Chapters 4 and 5 we'll talk about customizing your presentations by discovering what your audience wants and needs, and how your product or idea will help them.

3. **Communicate with more power and persuasion.**
   No matter how good or awful a communicator you are currently, the FIRE-UP System can help you tailor your message to suit your audience and then communicate that message with power and persuasion. The good news is that there are only

a few things you need to focus on to do really great presentations. With a little work and a little patience, you'll develop patterns of powerful communication, and you'll find your confidence level will rise along with your abilities.

4. **Enjoy giving presentations more than ever.**
   I think everyone is a little nervous when they're asked to present. I'll admit that I don't always wake up in the morning and say, "Oh boy! I'm so glad I get to do a presentation today!" But I've learned how to get myself into an emotional state where I will enjoy speaking to any group.

   Being able to speak persuasively and to move others to action is a great feeling. It will help you expand your sense of who you are and your impact in every area of your life. Certainly, you still may feel a few butterflies in the pit of your stomach when you think of "public speaking," but they'll be the butterflies of excitement rather than fear. And once you step in front of your audience and focus all of your attention on communicating with them clearly and with passion, then you'll find your own version of the speaker's "zone," where time flies and words seem to come effortlessly and enjoyably.

To master the FIRE-UP System, we must begin by defining exactly what a powerful persuasive presentation is. Read on and you'll learn how to create the ultimate win-win for you and your audience!

Chapter 1 Highlights

- Anyone can learn to be a persuasive communicator.

- Your job as a presenter is to persuade your audience to *embrace your outcome.*

- Great presenters get their audiences fired up about the outcome that the presentation creates. But only when you are emotionally engaged *yourself* will you be able to move your audience.

- An effective presentation is simply a series of interesting, connected conversations. When in front of a group, speak to one person at a time in your audience.

- *Four major outcomes of this book:*
  1. Significantly improve your results as a persuasive presenter.
  2. Add more value to your audiences.
  3. Communicate with more power and persuasion.
  4. Enjoy giving presentations more than ever.

Chapter Two
What is a Powerful and Persuasive Presentation?

Think about the great speakers you have seen, or you've heard about from history. What do they have in common? What was it about them or their presentations that caused you to go, "Wow, that was great"? I've made a study of great speakers and presentations, and I believe that a powerful, persuasive presentation can be defined very simply.

> *A powerful and persuasive presentation moves the audience to take action toward a predefined outcome while maintaining high levels of integrity.*

Let's spend a few moments exploring that definition. A powerful presentation must move your audience emotionally. Every successful salesperson will tell you that logic can only go so far in persuading someone to buy. Emotion is what ultimately makes the sale. Therefore, in order for your presentation to cause your audience to take action, you must touch your audience's feelings. And that emotion begins within you. If you aren't feeling it, your audience won't either. Or even worse, if you are feeling disempowering emotions like fear, doubt or anxiety, your audience will start to experience those emotions in combination with your content and be repelled by them. *The most powerful presentations are transfers of empowering emotion from you to your audience.*

But just touching people's feelings isn't enough: the audience must be moved to take *action*. Otherwise all you've done is to entertain your audience, and that's not persuasion. The emotion you create in your audience must be focused on a goal of creating some kind of decision or movement in their minds and hearts.

Cicero and Demosthenes were two great orators of the ancient world. When people heard Cicero, they would say, "What a wonderful speech!" But when people heard Demosthenes, they would say, "Let us march!" Demosthenes knew how to move his audience to take action.

It's also critical that you know *exactly* what you're moving your audience to do. Think about another great speaker, King Henry, from Shakespeare's play, *Henry V*. Henry was getting ready to lead his vastly outnumbered troops in a desperate battle against the French army. He had to inspire his men to fight despite horrible odds. But if he'd just fired his men up without knowing exactly what he wanted them to do, all the emotion and action Henry's words created wouldn't have achieved the goal of defeating the French. But because Henry had a clear, predetermined outcome, he was able to engage his army's emotions and get them to take action toward the outcome of winning the battle. And as a result, the English won the battle of Agincourt by beating an army ten times its size.

Henry's speech was clearly an example of a powerful, persuasive presentation. But there are far too many examples of other powerful and persuasive presentations in history that have produced devastating and horrible results. From all reports, Hitler and Mussolini were powerful and persuasive speakers. These men moved their audiences to take action toward very clear, predetermined outcomes. But no one I know wants to emulate these two horrific figures. Therefore, I believe that powerful and persuasive presentations must have high levels of *integrity*. Being a great presenter is not about manipulating your audience or getting people to do things that are unethical. The cost for that kind of presentation is always too high both for the audience and the presenter. Powerful and persuasive presentations must be based on your commitment to be honest, truthful, and true to your values, and to lead your audience to be true to their values as well.

Part of any presenter's commitment to integrity must include a focus on what's right for the audience first. If you stand in front of a group to sell a new software system, for instance, and you know your system won't do what they need it to, how can your presentation be based in integrity? How can you be honest or truthful with your audience? And would you be leading your audience with integrity if you sell them a system they don't need and can't use?

A persuasive and powerful presentation must have as its goal an outcome that will be a win for both sides. Not getting the sale wouldn't be a win for you; selling this company something they can't use wouldn't be a win for them. The best way to present with integrity is to know that your predetermined outcome will be a win for both sides. Remember King Henry? His outcome was to have his troops beat the French. That victory was absolutely vital for him and his country. He also knew that his troops were more likely to survive despite the odds if they were inspired to fight. So his goal in speaking to his troops was to create a win for him and for his army-in this case, a literal victory. Therefore Henry could speak with complete honesty and integrity as he inspired his men to attack the French. When you know that what you have to say is based on integrity, that you are being honest and truthful with your audience, that you are interested in their values and their well-being, then it becomes far easier to speak from the heart, to create emotion in your audience, and to move them to take action toward an outcome that will serve them.

Here's a checklist for the characteristics of a powerful and persuasive presentation. It . . .

1. Moves your audience emotionally.
2. Causes them to take action.
3. Has an outcome (predetermined by you) that is clear and specific.
4. Is in alignment with your values and the values of your audience, and creates a win on both sides.
5. Allows you to speak honestly, truthfully, and with integrity.

The Four Levels of Presentations

All of us know when we've seen a great presentation, and many of us probably have suffered through a poor one. But what's the difference between the two? When I teach persuasive presentations, I use a rating system based on something I heard once from Sergeant Bill Dower of the U.S. Marine Corps. Sergeant Dower was a decorated Marine veteran of the Vietnam War, and he became one of the Corps' top drill sergeants-in fact, he trained other Marines to be drill sergeants. Sergeant Dower is a powerful and persuasive speaker. Since he retired from the Marine Corps, he goes into high schools and speaks to young people, helping them to turn their lives around.

Sergeant Dower used to say there were four levels of performance: poor, good, excellent, and outstanding. I took these levels and applied them to the presentations I was observing in corporations and groups. Based on what I saw, about 25 percent of presentations were classified as poor. There was no outcome to the presentation; the presenter was in a terrible state and wasn't prepared; there was no connection established with the audience; the presenter didn't make sense or was dishonest . . . basically, the presenter did none of the things we listed as the qualities of a powerful, persuasive presentation.

About 50 percent of presentations would be considered good or average. The presenter was "good enough" but not really good. He or she did things the way everyone else does them, but there was no compelling outcome to the talk. There was some preparation, but the presenter was just speaking to a group of people rather than creating a series of connected conversations. The "good enough" presentation is more of a trap than the poor presentation because it gets us "some" results. That's why there are so many "good" presenters but very few excellent or outstanding ones. (I hope that if you're reading this book, you're not willing to settle for being just a "good" presenter!)

Excellent presentations make up about 15 to 20 percent of the total. Excellent presenters do many of the things listed earlier. They prepare themselves with both logic and emotion. They connect with their audience and keep their attention. They have a specific outcome. The structure of the presentation is clear and compelling. Their audience leaves saying, "That was a great presentation!" But... there's still a higher level when it comes to persuasive presentations: the level of outstanding. Like Demosthenes, Henry the Fifth, or Sergeant Bill Dower, the outstanding presenter connects with the audience in a deep, emotional way while also being in alignment with the audience's values and integrity. Outstanding presenters are completely prepared and absolutely "tuned in" to their audiences. They have an outcome that is absolutely compelling, both for them and for the people they address. Such presenters don't just impress an audience: they move that audience to action.

To deliver an outstanding presentation, you must change the audience's emotional state in relationship to the solution you provide and move them to take action on it!

The 5 to 10 percent of presentations that fall into the category of outstanding are the presentations and presenters that get 90 percent of the results.

I want you to decide right now what level of presentation you are committed to achieving. Hopefully you want to be better than poor—but will you settle for being "good enough"? Do you want to put in the effort to become excellent? Or are you willing to lay it on the line and decide that you won't settle for anything less than *outstanding*? Because that is the model this book is based upon. If you put the FIRE-UP System into practice, you absolutely can become an outstanding presenter. But you must commit to doing the work.

And you must be willing to break out of what's expected of you, or what you think you need to do as a presenter. In the corporate world I hear so many people complain about the poor quality of the presentations they see, yet they're suspicious of anything that breaks out of the "good enough" versions they've come to expect. In one of my recent presentations seminars in Europe, I had a student who was a government official. I was talking about how to connect more with your audience, and how to be enjoyable and entertaining as a presenter. But this gentleman interrupted me, saying, "That's not the way it's done in government. If you give a presentation like that, no one will believe you." Almost every suggestion I made about connecting with your audience, this gentleman would respond with, "No one in government would listen to you if you did that." Finally I asked him how he knew that was true, and he told me about a woman who had done a presentation for his government group. The woman was entertaining and kept everyone's attention, but afterwards the group's chairman called the presentation "amusing." Needless to say, the woman didn't move her audience to take action.

I said to this gentleman, "Since I wasn't there, I can't tell you what this woman did. I've seen presenters who are amusing and theatrical but don't really connect with the audience. And obviously her presentation didn't meet the criteria of moving her audience to act. But I believe that a truly powerful and persuasive presentation will work in almost every circumstance. Sure, you may have to tailor your *style* to suit different groups. I talk to a European audience a little differently than I do to an American one, or an Australian one, or one from the Far East. But I am always looking for ways to connect with this particular audience, to build an emotional bridge between them and me, to find out what their values are and align my presentation with them, and to move that audience to take action in accordance with those values." Once the gentleman saw how he could do that "in government," his presentations greatly improved.

To become an outstanding presenter, you've got to be willing to do what other people aren't. You've got to step outside of what you think a presenter "should" do in your industry, or in a particular situation. After fifteen years of training presenters, I have found that the principles of outstanding presentations are universal, whether you're speaking to your kids' Little League team or an audience of ten thousand conventioneers or the most straitlaced bunch of government officials in the world. But the only way you'll verify their universality is to learn and apply these principles yourself. In the next several chapters you'll find these principles laid out for you, but it's up to you to apply them with courage, dedication, and a sense of fun and exploration. Experiment with the ideas in this book. Play around with them in front of people you trust and see how much better your presentations are as a result.

Chapter 2 Highlights

A powerful, persuasive presentation moves the audience to take action toward a predefined outcome while maintaining high levels of integrity.

A powerful and persuasive presentation . . .
- Moves your audience emotionally.
- Causes them to take action: creating some kind of decision or movement in their minds and hearts.
- Has an outcome (predetermined by you) that is clear and specific.
- Is in alignment with your values and the values of your audience, and creates a win on both sides.
- Allows you to speak honestly, truthfully, and with integrity.

The four levels of presentations are:
1. Poor (25 percent): no outcome, presenter in terrible state, no connection with audience
2. Good or average (50 percent): presenter did what everyone else does; no compelling outcome, some preparation, presenter speaking to group rather than individuals; no real connection
3. Excellent (15 to 20 percent): presenter prepared with both logic and emotion; connects with audience, has a specific outcome, presentation clear and compelling
4. Outstanding (5 to 10 percent): presenter connects with audience in deep, emotional way; in alignment with audience's values; completely prepared; outcome is compelling; move audience to action.

Chapter Three
Climbing the Ladder of Outstanding Presentations

Now you know what a powerful and persuasive presentation is, and about the four levels of presentations—poor, good, excellent, and outstanding. You've committed to being one of the top "ten percenters" when it comes to presenting: you want nothing less than outstanding results. Now you're ready to start the work it will require to become the best of the best!

There are four major components of preparation for delivering an outstanding presentation.

1. Focus on your outcome.
2. Prepare yourself.
3. Communicate with integrity and power.
4. FIRE-UP your audience to achieve your outcome.

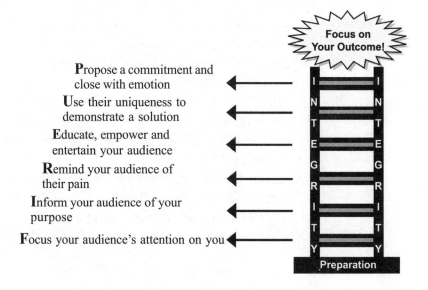

Focus on Your Outcome!

Propose a commitment and close with emotion ◄————

Use their uniqueness to demonstrate a solution ◄————

Educate, empower and entertain your audience ◄————

Remind your audience of their pain ◄————

Inform your audience of your purpose ◄————

Focus your audience's attention on you ◄————

INTEGRITY

Preparation

Four components should be easy to remember, right? But I have found that people find these components a lot easier to apply when I use a metaphor to describe how the process of creating and delivering a persuasive presentation works. So here it is: the ladder you and your audience will climb as you deliver outstanding presentations!

There are many reasons a ladder is a great metaphor for creating and delivering outstanding presentations. Almost everyone's been on a ladder at one time or another. A ladder helps you get from point A to point B. A ladder isn't the end result but a tool; it isn't the goal, but the means by which you reach a goal. We often use a ladder when we want to get to something that's out of reach based on where we are at the moment. And a ladder is a sturdy, clear path that we can take, step by step, to achieve what we want.

Each part of the ladder works in terms of the four major components of persuasive presentations. Sitting on top of the ladder is our *outcome*. If we don't focus on our outcome while we use the ladder, we won't know if the ladder is taking us where we want to go. The base of the ladder rests on the foundation of our *preparation*. If you've ever tried to put a ladder on a hill, soft dirt, or any other foundation that was less than firm, you know how difficult it is. When we prepare ourselves, however, the ladder of our presentation is grounded, solid, and steady.

The side rails of the ladder define our integrity. This means doing the right thing for your audience and staying true to your values as you communicate. These guide our steps toward our outcome and enable us to *communicate with integrity and power*. As long as we stay within our values, making the climb is easy. If we attempt to stray outside our values, we find ourselves treading on thin air, with no support and no way of reaching our goal.

Finally, each of the rungs of the ladder are steps for delivering the content of our presentation and get us to our outcome of persuading the audience to take action. Each of the six steps is represented by one letter of the word "FIRE-UP." Just like the rungs of a ladder, each step is an intermediate goal you must achieve on your way to your outcome. If you miss one, you risk falling off the ladder. But if you take each step in turn, reaching your goal will seem natural and almost effortless.

We will use this ladder metaphor as our guide for the rest of this book. In the chapters that follow you'll learn . . .

- How to create a clear, compelling outcome for each presentation and each audience;
- How to prepare yourself physically and emotionally to deliver the most outstanding presentation possible, and how to access that state at a moment's notice;
- How to discover your audience's wants, needs, and wounds;
- How to prepare yourself and your space on the day of your presentation;
- How to discover your values and the values of your audience, and use those values as the guide for your content;
- The secrets of powerful communicators the world over; and,
- The six steps of the Fire-UP ladder;
  - **F**ocus your audience's attention
  - **I**nform your audience of your purpose
  - **R**emind them of their pain
  - **E**ducate, empower, and entertain
  - **U**se their uniqueness to demonstrate a solution to their problem
  - **P**ropose a commitment and close with emotion.

But no ladder in the world will help you if you don't know where you want to go. So let's begin with focusing on the outcome for our presentation!

Chapter 3 Highlights

The four components of outstanding presentations are:
1. Focus on your outcome.
2. Prepare yourself.
3. Communicate with integrity and power.
4. FIRE-UP your audience to achieve your outcome.

     * We use a ladder metaphor to remind us of where we want to go, what we need as a foundation, the values that hold our presentation together, and the steps we must climb in succession to reach our outcome.

The six steps of the Fire-UP ladder are:
- **F**ocus your audience's attention
- **I**nform your audience of your purpose
- **R**emind them of their pain
- **E**ducate, empower, and entertain
- **U**se their uniqueness to demonstrate a solution to their problem
- **P**ropose a commitment and close with emotion.

Chapter Four
Know Where Your Ladder Leads:
Focus on Your Outcome

I once saw a silent comedy film in which a man was carrying a tall ladder from one place to another. He was staggering around helplessly, trying to balance the ladder from the bottom while the top waved madly through the air. It was a funny image, but it's very accurate when it comes to the FIRE-UP ladder of persuasive presentations. You can do a great job of preparing your talk, building your case, and staying true to your values, but if don't know where your ladder is supposed to take you-your outcome-you're in trouble. Just as a ladder is useless unless it takes you from where you are to where you want to go, a presentation is useless unless it has an outcome.

I'm a member of the board of advisors for a company in the Seattle, Washington area, and a few years ago I was on a harbor cruise the company held for their investors. The management team was going to do a presentation during the cruise, and about ten minutes before they were scheduled to start, the president of the company came up to me and said, "Tom, you do a lot of presentations-would you mind saying a few words to get us started?" Now, I'm a professional speaker, and I didn't want to beg off and say "I can't, I'm unprepared," so I agreed. But for the next few minutes I was really struggling. I felt uncertain, even nervous, wondering what in the world I was going to talk about for five minutes-me, the professional! Finally, I realized my problem: I didn't know my outcome. I went to the president and asked, "When I'm done with these five minutes, what do you want to make sure I've accomplished?" Once I knew the outcome, I was able to come up with a message that met the president's outcome.

Having a clear outcome is the foundation of every powerful presentation because it focuses all your resources in one direction. If you don't have an outcome, you're going to get nervous and struggle, and your mind is going to wander. Your presentation will lack focus and clarity, and then you'll lose your audience as well. Defining a clear, focused outcome for your presentation is the most important thing you can do long before you ever step in front of a group.

I define outcome as the *end result* of your presentation, and the end result must be an *action* you wish your audience to take. What do you want your audience to do? In my presentation seminars people sometimes tell me, "My outcome is to educate my audience." That's great—but unless you're a teacher, education is not an outcome. *Action* is. Persuasion is the process of moving people toward a specific result, which almost always is an action of some kind. If you can put your outcome in terms of an action, I guarantee you'll find it much easier to be persuasive, compelling, and powerful as a presenter.

Suppose you have to introduce your idea for a new product or service to your company's executive management team. If you created a presentation with the outcome of educating the team about your idea, they could learn all about it and still tell you no. But if your outcome was "to move them to enthusiastically adopt this idea and to give it their full support," how much more focused would your presentation become? It would be far easier for you to decide what to include, what to eliminate, and what to emphasize. More important, you'll probably be a much more exciting speaker, because the second outcome is designed to involve you emotionally as well as intellectually. And since all presentations are transfers of emotion, the more emotionally involved you are in your outcome the easier it will be for you to move your audience emotionally as well.

How do you create an outcome? You can begin by thinking about your presentation, your audience, and your own goals. Ask yourself questions like, "What's the outcome of this presentation? Why am I going to get up and talk? When I'm done, what's the result I wish to achieve? What do I want my audience to be thinking? What do I want them talking about? And most important, what actions do I want them to take?" Later in this chapter I'll give you some guidelines for creating clear, specific, focused, emotionally-involving outcomes. However, there's an even easier way to determine your outcome: ask someone who represents the needs and wishes of your audience.

What Does Your Audience Want and Need?

Imagine you want to buy a new home and you need to choose a realtor to help you in your search. The first realtor you visit doesn't ask you a single question. Instead, she pulls out the plans for a new development in your city and says, "I have the perfect home for you!" Only one small problem: she shows you a one-bedroom townhouse when you have three kids and a dog. When you mention this to her, she says, "Well, this is what I show all my customers." You say thank you and get out of her office as quickly as possible.

The next realtor couldn't be more different. Instead of pulling out pictures of homes, she tells you, "Before I show you anything, I'd like you to describe for me exactly what you want and need in a home. If you could have the perfect home, what would it look like and where would it be? I'd also like to know why you want to move-is there something you don't like about your current house?" Only after she is completely clear on what you are looking for does she show you anything, and as a result the houses she shows you fill your needs perfectly.

When you are preparing a presentation, most of the time you can do exactly what the second realtor did: ask your audience prior to your presentation to help you create a clear and specific outcome. The leader of the group you will be speaking to can be a great ally in determining your outcome. If you've been invited to give a presentation to the customer service department, for instance, ask the department manager. If you're going into a company to do a presentation about your consulting services, ask a senior executive about the company's goals. If you're speaking to an industry group, ask the person who contacted you to speak (as long as that person is a member of the industry group, too). You want to get your information from the best source possible.

As a presenter, I believe it's critical for me to know three things about any audience or group.

1. **What is the outcome for this particular group?** Where does this group want to end up in terms of this particular issue? If I'm doing a training for a team of sales executives, for instance, I'd want to know what they would consider the outcome of the class. Does the team want to improve their presentation skills? Close more customers? Be better at leading sales teams? Those are all very different outcomes, and I would need to shape my presentation accordingly.

2. **Where is this group currently in relation to this topic or area?** Sometimes I do trainings for executives who simply want to upgrade their speaking skills. Other times I'm working with people who are terrified of public speaking. The outcome of my presentation definitely will be affected by where the group sees itself in relation to its ultimate goal. You also need to know how far your audience believes it will have to travel to reach the outcome. If you're walking into an organization where two departments see themselves as completely at odds, and your job is to offer communications training, your approach will be very different than if you're leading a weekend workshop to help successful customer service people do an even better job on the phones.

3. **What are the obstacles keeping this group from where it wants to go?** Obstacles can take many forms: outdated systems, people who are afraid to

change, company culture, industry-wide challenges, even the current economic climate. Your presentation needs to take into account whatever the group believes is getting in the way of their outcome. Otherwise, you run the risk of looking like you haven't done your homework, and people will tend to discount what you have to say even if it has merit. (You especially need to know if some of the people in the audience would be considered among the obstacles!)

When I'm scheduled to speak to a company or group, I usually contact the group's leader at least three to four weeks before the date of my presentation. I ask the following questions:

- What are your expectations of this presentation?
- What's the result you want to get from this session?
- What problems do you want to solve?
- What does your group want and/or need in terms of this area?
- Where are you now in terms of this result?
- What are the obstacles keeping you from where you want to go? What do you believe is keeping you from getting this result so far?
- Are there people in the audience or in the company who aren't fans of this?
- Are there things about the company, industry, or economic climate that I need to know?
- When I'm done, what do you want to make sure I've covered?
- Is there anything else unique about this group that would help me tailor my presentation to your needs?

Most people are thrilled to spend a few minutes explaining what they want from a presentation. By asking the leader for information about the group's needs, wants, and problems, you will be demonstrating a level of caring and dedication to the customer that will put you head and shoulders above the rest.

Make Sure You're the Right Person for the Job

Going back to our realtor example, what if you were looking for a single-family house on an acre of land and you went to a realtor who specialized in townhouses and condos? Would that realtor be the best person to help you find the house you want? Probably not. The same is true when giving presentations. If you specialize in executive management skills training, for example, and someone wants you to come in and train salespeople on closing more customers, you might not be the best person for the job. This kind of situation happens frequently to presenters and trainers: do a great job of training one group or department and you may very well be asked to do the same for another group, even if your material may not be well-suited to the second group's needs.

Whenever possible, make sure that you are the right person to assist this particular group in getting their outcome. If you're not and you take on the job anyway, make sure that you've earned the right to talk about the subject you've been asked to discuss by immersing yourself in the subject. If you're not a financial person and you're going to be presenting to the accounting department, you'd better get very familiar with accounting terminology as well as the problems faced by this specific department. If you come from the world of finance and you're going to be talking to salespeople, you'd better know a lot about sales techniques, closing ratios, and how salespeople succeed.

Obviously you can't become an expert in the fields of every group you speak to, but you need to be familiar enough with the background, technology, concerns, and expertise of your audience so they will be willing to listen to what you have to say. Most important of all, you need to get excited about how your material can help the people in this audience. Sometimes the most innovative ideas and solutions occur when someone with a different expertise brings a new perspective into a challenging situation and helps an audience to see things in a new light.

Before accepting a speaking assignment, ask yourself two questions. First, do I have the right to talk about this subject to this audience, and if not, what will I commit to learn so that the audience and I feel that I have the right? Second, am I excited about this subject and eager to share it with other people? If not, what do I need to do to get excited? If you can't get excited about the subject or you aren't willing to do what it takes to master at least the basics of the field, then perhaps you should pass up the assignment.

However, I believe one of the greatest gifts of being a speaker is the opportunity to expand my own knowledge by familiarizing myself with new areas of expertise. I have learned a great deal about different businesses, social groups, subjects, and disciplines so I could stand in front of my audience and speak with authority. If you take the time and effort to do the same, you not only will be a persuasive presenter but you will become a more knowledgeable person in the process.

The Seven Characteristics of a Powerful Outcome

I tell people to write down the outcome for every presentation they do. Yes, every presentation! Writing the outcome makes you distill it to its essence, which then allows you to keep the outcome in mind while you are making the presentation. Your written outcome should be put into very specific terms, and designed to solve the problem and/or fill the wants and needs of my audience.

There are seven characteristics of a powerful and effective outcome. It must be:

1. **Specific as to the result you desire.** An unclear outcome will mean an unclear presentation. What specific action do you want your audience to be moved to take?

2. **Brief and to the point.** Keep it simple—one or two sentences max. Your outcome should be something you can keep in your mind throughout your presentation.

3. **Written in the positive.** A negative outcome rarely produces positive results. If your outcome is to help this company never lose another customer, great-but how are you going to do that? A better way to state the outcome might be "the sales team created raving fans of customers by exceeding customers' service expectations." Stating your outcome in the positive helps you get very clear on the specific action you wish your audience to take.

4. **Written in the past tense.** When you write an outcome in the past tense, you're telling your brain it has already happened. In essence, you're creating in advance the future you want to occur.

5. **Focused on solving problems and significantly improving your audience's business or situation.** Every outcome must offer a solution and fill the wants and needs of this particular group. How will the lives of this group be better if this outcome is achieved? Providing a solution for a group's problems is the surest way to move them to take action. Remember, your outcome has nothing to do with you and everything to do with your audience. Your outcome should describe the audience having their problems solved by taking an action that utilizes the solution you have provided.

6. **Energizing and exciting.** If your outcome isn't passionate, you won't be either. Avoid weak or fuzzy words; instead, use terms you can get excited about. No one is going to see this but you, so you can use

any words you want as long as they energize you. Your outcome should be so inspiring that if you woke up the morning of your presentation and just didn't feel motivated, you could look at your outcome and say, "Oh yeah-that's why I'm doing this!" and jump out of bed raring to go.

7. **Something you are committed to and driven to achieve.** Remember Sergeant Bill Dower? He exemplifies the kind of commitment and drive your outcome should produce inside of you. You should feel like you're on a mission to achieve this outcome, that it's so important you'd go through a wall for it.

A clear, focused, exciting outcome can be the one element that makes or breaks your presentation. It's like the tipping point: having a clear outcome tips the presentation in the direction of enormous momentum and excitement. Without it, creating any kind of momentum is an enormous struggle. With a clear outcome, the smallest effort creates far greater results, because you've got a clear channel through which the energy of your presentation can flow.

A few years ago a professional speaker in Australia asked me to coach her. Her topic was "Dress for Success." She'd been speaking about it for years and had done very well, but she noticed that lately her audiences weren't responding and she wasn't getting asked to speak as often. She thought she needed help with her presenting, but the real problem was that she wasn't emotionally excited about her topic anymore. She thought "Dress for Success" was passé, that it wasn't changing people's lives.

The first thing we did was to change the outcome of her presentations. For her to be effective, she had to sell herself on the fact that she was having an impact on people's lives. She created an outcome based around the idea that dressing for success was the one thing that could make the difference between a job and a rejection, a promotion and being passed over, feeling good about yourself and feeling like a faceless entity in a cubicle. "What you wear and how you look will give you the edge!" was her new slogan. Her audiences responded, she got more bookings, and now she's busier and more successful than ever.

Remember, a presentation is ultimately a transfer of emotions. You've got to have some excitement about your topic within you if you're going to be effective. If your outcome is dynamic, exciting, and solution-oriented, then your presentation will be, too.

There's a beautiful example of the power of a clear, focused, compelling outcome in the movie *Braveheart*. In the key battle scene, the Scots were looking across a field at the English army. The English outnumbered the Scots and were far better armed and trained. The Scots hesitated, not knowing quite what to do. One man rode up and said, "This is crazy, maybe we should go back!" But his manner and voice made it clear he was as uncertain as the rest of the Scots. Then the leader of the Scots, William Wallace, rode up. He knew his outcome: he wanted a free Scotland for these men and their families. It was clear from his voice and his body that this vision was something he was excited about and completely committed to. He told the Scots, "Today you may die, but you're going to die free men, in the service of a great cause. They can take our lives, but they can never take our freedom!" And the Scots charged into battle. Because William Wallace had a clear, compelling, focused outcome of freeing his country and its people from the English-an outcome he was willing to give his life for—he was able to move men to act against impossible odds.

Exercise: Creating a Compelling Outcome

1. Choose a persuasive presentation opportunity you will be facing in the next few weeks.
   Example: Your consulting firm has been asked to develop and present a new software delivery tracking system for ABC

Company. In two weeks you have to present your plan to ABC's board.

_____

_____

_____

2. Write down the primary problems, wants, and needs of the group you will be speaking to.
   Example:
   Primary problems: Wasting millions of dollars on inefficient processes. Significant downtime with their current technology solution.
   Wants: To reduce their costs and improve the efficiency of their systems.
   Needs: To deliver products more quickly to their customers. To be able to provide better service at less cost. To stand out from their competition and be recognized as a leader in their area.

_____

_____

_____

_____

_____

_____

_____

_____

3. Based on this group's problems, wants and needs, write the outcome you want in that situation using the seven characteristics of a compelling outcome as described earlier. What result do you want for your audience from this presentation?

    Example: ABC Company implemented our state of the art software delivery tracking system that dramatically reduced their cost of business. Our solution along with our ongoing commitment to their success enabled ABC to significantly improve their productivity and profitability, and become an industry leader in the process.

    _____

    _____

    _____

    _____

    _____

    _____

    _____

    _____

    _____

    _____

    _____

Once you know where your ladder is taking you—your outcome—you are ready to do the groundwork that will give your presentation the firm foundation it needs to allow you to climb to the top!

Chapter 4 Highlights

To create and deliver a persuasive presentation, you must know your outcome: the end result of your presentation, which is an action you wish your audience to take. Create your outcome by thinking about your presentation, your audience, and your goals.

Discover what your audience wants and needs by asking the three questions of leader of the group you will be addressing.
   A. What is the outcome for this particular group? Where does this group want to end up in terms of this particular issue?
   B. Where is this group currently in relation to this topic or area?
   C. What are the obstacles keeping this group from where it wants to go?

Make sure you're the right person for this particular presentation. Before accepting a speaking assignment, ask yourself:
   1. Do I have the right to talk about this subject to this audience? And if not, what will I commit to study, learn, or master so the audience and I feel that I have the right?
   2. Am I excited about this subject and eager to share it with other people? If not, what do I need to do to get excited?

A powerful and effective outcome must be . . .
   • Specific as to the result you desire.
   • Brief and to the point.
   • Written in the positive.
   • Written in the past tense.
   • Focused on solving problems and significantly improving your audience's business or situation.
   • Energizing and exciting.
   • Something you are committed to and driven to achieve.

Chapter Five
Create a Rock Solid Foundation:
Prepare Yourself-Phase One

Have you ever tried to climb a ladder that was planted in soft ground? The ladder can shift unexpectedly and throw you off-balance, making it difficult for you to reach your objective. No matter how strong the ladder or how clear your objective, your ladder needs to be standing on solid ground. Preparation gives the ladder of your presentation the foundation it needs for you to be successful.

There are many elements that go into preparing for a persuasive presentation. Creating an outcome, as we discussed in Chapter 4, is a key element. Knowing your particular audience—their wants, needs, and problems—is also essential. Then there are the obvious parts of preparation: determining your content, getting your handouts, slides, or other visual elements ready, and so on. I call all of this Phase One of your preparation. But there's another area that far too many presenters neglect: making sure you're in the right physical, mental, and emotional state. And Phase Two of your preparation is just as important as Phase One.

In this chapter we'll explore Phase One of creating a solid foundation for your presentation so you can reach your outcome in the most effective way. While preparation isn't glamorous, it will make you a more comfortable and dynamic speaker. You may also find it enjoyable, as you discover more about your audience *and* learn how to access your most resourceful and powerful emotions on command!

Get to Know Your Audience

Phase One begins with *knowing your audience*. When you were formulating your outcome for the presentation, you should have been in touch with the group leader or contact person, to discover (1) the results the audience wants from your presentation, (2) their wants, needs, and problems, and (3) what obstacles they believe stand in their way in terms of their results. Based on what you discovered, you should have come up with a specific outcome.

But as part of your preparation, it's good to check back with the group to see if your outcome is on track. If possible, I like to do a pre-presentation call with any key people in the group I'll be speaking to. I'll say, "Based on our prior conversations and what I understand as the needs of your group, I believe your outcome for this presentation is X. Is that accurate? Do you have any suggestions or changes you feel I should make to that outcome?" This kind of call can make for a much more satisfied audience and a much easier job for you as the presenter.

Far too often an executive will call a speaker or outside consultant and say, "I need someone to come in and talk on this topic"–for example, sales, leadership, or customer retention. The consultant arrives thinking he or she knows the outcome of the speech, but there's no clarity about the specific outcome of this particular group. Persuasive presenters customize their presentations towards their specific audience. They do a different presentation for ABC Company than for XYZ Company, based on the company's specific needs.

Calling the group leader to check on your outcome also gives you an opportunity to *ask any additional questions that will help you become even more familiar with the group* and the challenges they are facing in relation to your outcome.

I especially like to discover what motivates this particular group, so that I can make sure my presentation will move them to take action. (The goal of every persuasive presentation, remember?) The questions I ask are designed to discover the following motivating factors.

- **Concerning this situation, what do they find painful?** Are they not meeting sales quotas? Are they under pressure from their bosses? Do they feel they aren't meeting the customers' needs? Are they losing customers? Do they feel unsupported by other departments in the company, or by each other? I try to discover what is causing them the most pain in this situation, so I can show them a solution that will not just solve their problem but also relieve their pain.

- **Concerning this situation, what do they associate pleasure to?** Do they feel good about their teammates, or about carrying on despite tremendous odds? Are they generally happy with the way things are, if only this one thing was changed? Knowing what a group feels good about already will help you (1) increase the pleasure they already have, and (2) ensure that any changes/ solution you propose will let them keep what enjoyment they have or give them something that they will find equally or more pleasurable.

- **What potential objections might they have to the outcome or solution I am proposing?** For instance, if you're suggesting a long and expensive sales training for a group that already feels stretched thin time—and money-wise, then unless you eliminate their objections you're unlikely to get the group's agreement. Make sure you ask this question of the group leader so you can uncover objections and either (1) change your outcome or (2) handle the objections up front.

- **What are the characteristics and backgrounds of the people who will be attending the presentation?** The more you know about your audience, the easier it will be to "hit them where they live." There's nothing more effective than being able to incorporate specific details about your audience into your presentation.

Once you've gathered as much information as you can from the group leader, and you've confirmed that your outcome for the presentation is on track, you're ready for the next step in your preparation: *become an expert on this particular topic and group.* You don't have to know everything, but you do need to know enough. Immerse yourself in what you're going to talk about. If you're already an expert in your field, you can always learn more. Make sure you're up to date on the latest advances in this industry.

To be a persuasive presenter you've got to believe in yourself, and part of that confidence comes with knowing that you've done your homework on your topic and your audience.

When you've gathered all the information you need about the group and about this particular topic, you're ready to *set the content of your presentation using the "rungs" of the FIRE-UP ladder.* (We'll describe these rungs in Chapters 9 through 14.) When you work on your content, I suggest that you create an outline or series of bullet points rather than writing every word of your talk. Using an outline to remind you of the points you want to make, the stories and examples you want to use, and the amount of time you want to spend on each section will help you keep on track while allowing you to talk to people rather than at them. You can use a written or typed outline, a PowerPoint slide, or any other method that works for you. The key is to break your talk into "chunks" so that you can look at one or two words and have them trigger what you want to say for the next few minutes.

When it comes to creating their content, many beginning presenters will ask me two questions: (1) How do you know how much time you'll need for a speech? (2) How do you know how much content to cram into a specific time frame? I follow the guidance of Albert Einstein, who said, "Make things as simple as

FIRE-UP Outline

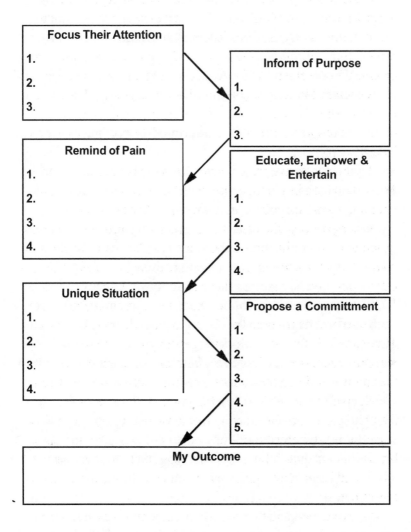

possible, yet not any simpler." When you outline your content, make sure every part is something that moves people closer to the outcome of your presentation. Keep things simple and clear. If you need 25 minutes to accomplish your outcome, don't take thirty. Be ruthless. Many experienced presenters have a wealth of great stories on any number of subjects, and sometimes they include these stories even when the material is only marginally applicable to the outcome of the talk! Anything that doesn't directly lead your audience to your outcome must be considered fluff and should be eliminated.

Other presenters can try to cram three hours of material into a one-hour presentation. Don't do it. All you'll do is frustrate yourself and your audience. Make sure the outcome you set can be accomplished in the time you have. If you have to make your outcome more specific in order to get it done during the course of your presentation, do so. It's far better to succeed completely in getting a more specific outcome than to succeed only partly in getting the too-big outcome you originally set.

Let's take a concrete example. Suppose you've been asked to give a presentation about a brand-new computer software program to a large company. You've been told you have exactly one hour. You've been working on this computer software for over a year and you know every bell and whistle in the program and how it will increase the company's productivity by 40 percent. But you also know that to teach them how to use the program to its fullest would require four to eight hours of concentrated training.

Some presenters might set as their outcome, "To inform the management team about this program so they'll see how great it is." With that outcome, they would try and cram as much information as they could into that hour, going over all the program's tricks and secrets and thoroughly confusing their audience. But is that outcome achievable in an hour? Not realistically. What would be a better outcome? "The management team chose to significantly increase their productivity by purchasing our software program."

An outcome like this is easily achievable in the time allotted and is more likely to result in a win for both presenter and audience.

Once your content is outlined, you're ready to create or gather any support materials you may need: PowerPoint slides, handouts, samples, any other audio-visual elements, and so on. Again, remember to include only materials that support your outcome. You may be doing a presentation that you've done before, and the presentation has fifty PowerPoint slides. But each time you should go through every single slide and ask, "Does this support the outcome for this group?" If you only need twenty of the slides, use twenty.

Nowadays you can pull outlines and materials for corporate presentations off the Internet. That's fine—as long as you edit the materials with an eye toward your specific outcome. The worst thing you can do as a presenter is to appear "canned" or as if this is a generic speech you do for every group. Coming up with a specific outcome based on the group's needs and making sure all your content and support materials tie into that outcome will make you a more persuasive and effective presenter.

The final part of Phase One is to *make sure any other team members involved in your presentation are fully up to speed in terms of the outcome and the content elements.* In today's corporate world, it's becoming more and more usual for people to present as a team. If this is the case, it's important to include other team members in all aspects of preparation. Make them aware of the outcome of the presentation and their role in achieving it. If you are the main presenter, you are responsible for what your team members say or do not say. It's to your benefit to make sure everyone on your team is properly prepared.

Now that you've done all of your physical preparation, you're clear on your outcome, and you've checked it with the group you will be presenting to, you're ready for the most important part of preparation: getting yourself ready physically and emotionally to deliver the goods.

Chapter 5 Highlights

- Phase One of your preparation begins with knowing your audience. Check back with the group leader to see if your outcome is on track. Ask questions that will help you to discover what motivates this particular company or group, such as:
    - Concerning this situation, what does this group find painful?
    - What do they associate pleasure to in this situation?
    - What potential objections might they have to the outcome or solution I am proposing?
    - What are the characteristics and backgrounds of the people who will be attending the presentation?

- Become an expert on this particular topic and group. Study the field and the company. Make sure you are up to date on the latest industry advances.

- Once you've gathered all the information you need, set the content of your presentation using the FIRE-UP! ladder rungs described in Chapters 9 through 14. Create an outline or series of bullet points rather than writing out every word of your talk. Be concise.

- Once your content is outlined, create or gather any support materials you may need: PowerPoint slides, handouts, samples, etc. Include only materials that support your outcome.

- Make sure any other team members involved in your presentation are fully up to speed about your outcome and content elements.

Chapter Six
Create a Rock Solid Foundation:
Prepare Yourself—Phase Two

If a presentation is a transfer of emotion from speaker to audience, and a persuasive presentation moves the audience to take action on a predetermined outcome, it makes sense that you need access to your emotions in order to transfer them to an audience, right? And to move an audience to take action, you must tap into your own mental and emotional power. You must be at the top of your game whenever you are in front of a group, and that's why Phase Two is *mental and emotional preparation.* You can have the greatest outcome and content in the world, but if you don't prepare mentally and emotionally long before you stand in front of the audience, your delivery of the content will suffer, and you probably won't achieve your outcome.

Mental and emotional preparation starts by defining what I call the **Optimal Performance Identity** (OPI) you will need to access to perform at your peak. Your OPI is a description of who you are as a presenter when you're at your best. Imagine watching a videotape of yourself giving the greatest presentation of your life—what inspiring words would you use to describe this person? Or suppose someone was writing a brochure about a remarkable presenter who got amazing results every single time—and that person was you. What would the brochure say? Here are four hints to give you a hand in constructing your own OPI:

1. **Think of a great presentation you did, and then describe yourself in terms of your emotions and outcome.** If you aren't an experienced presenter yet, think of someone you would like to emulate as a presenter and describe him/her. Then write your description in the first person, using "I" instead of "he" or "she."

2. **Make sure you describe both who you are and what you accomplish during the course of a presentation.** For example, "I'm an accomplished, dynamic presenter who moves my audience to action using every means at my disposal."

3. **Your description should excite you.** It's better to think big than small, to step out of your comfort zone rather than describe someone who is merely competent. Dream big in your OPI—no one will see it but you.

4. **Make sure your OPI is no longer than five or six sentences.** Your OPI is something you will be referring to whenever you give a presentation, so make it a statement you can remember with ease.

Here's an OPI I created several years ago, when I first began formulating the foundations for persuasive presentations:

"I am an outstanding presenter. I focus on my customers, and my content flows effortlessly. I create a series of interesting, connected conversations with each person in my audience. I use all my skills and I totally immerse myself in my presentation. I enjoy solving my audience's problems with solutions tailored to their specific needs. I always lead my customers to a powerful outcome. I love giving presentations and it shows in the way I present! This is who I am!"

I review my OPI every single time I am preparing a presentation, and I make adjustments based on the specific presentation I will be doing. Sometimes I make no adjustments at all; other times I will tweak one or two sentences. But my OPI always describes who I am and what I want to accomplish for this presentation, and it uses words that create feelings of excitement, enjoyment, and anticipation within me.

Exercise:

Using the four hints, write down your own OPI, making sure it is something that excites and motivates you as a presenter.

_____

_____

_____

_____

_____

_____

_____

_____

_____

_____

Your OPI Emotional Recipe

Everyone can give at least one great presentation. I'll bet if you had to speak on something you were truly passionate about—your family, your country, your beliefs, even a sports team you loved—you would do a great job. But people who give presentations as part of their livelihood must speak persuasively and passionately no matter how they're feeling. Persuasive presenters have to know how to "turn themselves on" in any situation, to engage emotion, mind, and body in the service of what they will say.

As a speaker, there are certain emotions that will help you be at your best. Think of great presenters you have seen. What emotions made them so effective? When I ask this question in my seminars, people usually come up with emotions like excitement, confidence, passion, conviction, humor, dedication, caring, compassion, honesty, daring, and fun.

Each person has a unique "recipe" of emotions that will help him or her to be an outstanding presenter. Content and outcomes may change, but a presenter's emotional recipe is usually consistent. That's why in addition to your OPI statement, you must define the OPI emotions you need to feel to perform at your peak as a presenter. Defining and then embodying your unique emotional OPI recipe whenever you speak will guarantee you consistently great results.

You define your OPI emotional recipe by identifying the emotions you need to access to deliver an outstanding presentation and achieve your outcome. Take a look at your OPI statement and ask yourself the following questions.

1. **To be this person and to accomplish the outcomes described in my OPI, what emotions will I need to access?** List all the emotions that would help you be a great presenter: confidence, excitement, humor, conviction, passion, daring, etc. Write these emotions as "I am" statements, for example, "I am confident," "I am humorous," or "I am passionate."

2. **Are there any emotions that I must get rid of?** Emotions like fear, anxiety, uncertainty, rigidity, and

lack of humor will inevitably cause problems. Your content can be great but, it won't matter, if your emotions get in the way of your delivering it effectively. As part of your preparation, you must get rid of these disempowering emotions.

I believe the most important emotion for a persuasive presenter is caring for your audience. I have seen presenters who use commands or demands to instill fear and browbeat the audience into taking action. But how long do you think browbeating, fear, or commands will motivate people? More important, is that the kind of presenter you wish to be?

I find many inexperienced presenters make three very common mistakes when it comes to connecting with the audience. First, they don't take the time to feel connected before they start. (In Chapter 7 we'll talk about a pre-speech routine that will help you do just that.) Second, they call upon emotions that really don't help them establish connection. Third, their outcome is focused on themselves, not their audience. If you truly want to persuade people and move them to action, they must feel that you care about their wants, needs, and problems, and that the outcome of your presentation is in their best interests.

While your list will undoubtedly be different, here is my current emotional OPI. I like pairing emotions because it gives me extra "oomph."

- *I am caring and connected.*
- *I am playful and having fun.*
- *I am certain and committed.*
- *I am centered and relaxed.*
- *I am energized and excited.*
- *I am adventurous and daring.*

Your own emotional recipe will evolve as you get in front of people. You'll notice when your recipe wasn't working, and you'll add emotions to make your presentations better. A few years ago I changed my own OPI emotions in response to feedback from my audience. People would tell me, "Great job, Tom! A little too intense, though." So I added "playful and fun" to my recipe, and my presentations improved markedly as a result. "Adventurous and daring" came later, when I found myself getting into a little bit of a rut as a presenter. It was easy for me to be confident, relaxed, funny, committed, and energized, but my excitement level was beginning to flag. (When you give a presentation on the same topic for the fiftieth time, you can get a bit stale!) But when I added "adventurous and daring" (even though those two emotions were a stretch for me), my excitement returned. I took more chances in my presentations. I challenged both myself and my audience to hold ourselves to higher standards. Simply adding these two emotions brought a new energy and freshness to my work. Today I feel that "adventurous and daring" are two of the most important qualities I can bring to any speech.

Some of the emotions in your OPI recipe will stretch you and move you out of your comfort zone. But, if you adopt these emotions, practice them, and make them part of who you are, then you will show up as the best person you can possibly be whenever you present. And those are the emotions that will be transferred to your audience and associated to your outcome.

Exercise:
1. Take a look at your OPI and, using the questions listed earlier, write down your own unique emotional recipe, making sure that it includes all the emotions you will need to be an outstanding presenter, including some form of caring or connection.

_____

_____

_____

2. List any emotions you need to eliminate because they may interfere with your being your best. You'll learn a method for eliminating these emotions at the end of this chapter.

_____

_____

_____

_____

_____

_____

_____

Accessing your OPI Emotions

Once you know your emotional OPI recipe, you need to make sure you can access these emotions easily. Every great presenter makes sure that they are in their OPI emotions for every presentation they give. Luckily, tapping into these emotions is easy, once you know how. To access our emotions, we will draw upon the research and expertise of psychologists and experts in the fields of physiology and neurobiology. For the last quarter century, these scientists have taught that emotions are created by very specific combinations of *mental focus and physical movement.*

Let me give you an example. Think about something depressing and notice what your body does. If you're like 99.9 percent of people, your shoulders slumped, your eyes focused downward, your mouth turned down, your breathing became shallow, and you felt a lack of energy throughout your body. Notice what you focused. What were you seeing? What did you hear, or what were you saying to yourself?

Now, get up from your chair or the sofa or wherever you're reading this book, and stand tall and strong. Throw your head back, put a big, silly grin on your face, and breathe deeply. Think about the funniest cartoon you ever saw. Hear the soundtrack or laugh track of that cartoon in your head. Now, as you keep standing, grinning, and thinking about the cartoon, try to be depressed. You can't do it! That's because every emotion we feel has a very specific combination of physical and mental elements. If you put together those physical and mental elements, you will feel the emotion whether there's any particular reason for it or not.

As presenters, we can use this fact to help us access the emotions we need to be at our best. We can use the information provided by **Neuro-Linguistic Programming (NLP)**—which describes how we communicate with ourselves and others—to get very specific when it comes to our own emotions. I learned from Anthony Robbins how to use the tools of NLP to build an emotion using the *Three Emotional Triggers:* (1) physiology, (2) language and submodalities, and (3) beliefs.

A trigger is something that allows you to access a thought, emotion, or physiology as soon as you fire it off. Using the triggers of physiology, language and submodalities, and empowering beliefs, you can access any emotion upon command. But first you have to discover your own formula for creating an emotion using these three elements.

Trigger #1: Physiology
Physiology is the way you use your body. In includes many different elements, but for our purposes the most important are:

- Posture
- Breathing
- Gestures/movement
- Facial expressions
- Muscle tension or relaxation

———————————○———————————

Every emotion we feel has a corresponding physiological pattern, composed of these elements. For example, happy people usually have an upright posture, their breathing is normal or a little fuller than normal, their heads are raised, they're looking straight ahead or a little up, their gestures and movements are animated, they're smiling, their eyebrows are up, and there's a sense of energy (but not excess tension) in the body.

Here's the secret of physiology: *If you adopt a physiology of a particular emotion, you will start to access that emotion automatically.* If you want to feel happy, adopt a happy posture. If you want to feel unstoppable, get your body into the physiology of unstoppableness. Actors and presenters use this secret all the time to access emotions upon command. It's the most effective way I know to get into your OPI emotions. Even if you have to do a presentation at the last minute, you can adopt the physiology of your OPI emotions and know you'll have access to those emotions immediately.

However, as all actors and presenters will tell you, to access your emotions at a moment's notice you first have to know your own specific physiological triggers for the different emotions. That means you need to put yourself into those emotional states in advance so you can discover your unique physiological formula for that emotion.

There are two simple and effective ways to discover the physiology of an emotion. (I suggest you find a time and place where you can be by yourself so you can do this exercise fully.) Begin by choosing the OPI emotion you want to access—for example, confidence.

1. Remember a time when you felt absolutely confident about something. In your mind, put yourself back into that situation. See what you were seeing, feel what you were feeling. Now, move your body into the posture you had when you were feeling confident. How were you standing? How were you breathing?

———————————●———————————

How did you move? What expression did you have on your face? Let yourself feel that confidence fully, and let your body do exactly what it did then.

2. Once you're fully in that confident state, notice what your body is doing and make specific notes about posture, breathing, gestures, facial expression, and the amount of muscle tension and/or relaxation you experience in different parts of your body.

If you can't remember a time when you felt this particular emotion, another method of discovering the physiology of a specific emotion—borrow the physiology from someone else.

1. Think of someone in your own life, or someone you've seen on TV or in the movies, that you feel has a lot of confidence. If it's someone you know, remember the specific occasion when he or she was exuding confidence. If it's someone from the movies or TV, remember the specific show or film.

2. Make a picture of this person in your mind, and look closely at the way this person uses his/her body. Note the posture, where the breath is, the gesture and movements, the facial expressions, the amount of muscle tension and/or relaxation in various parts of the body. Write down everything you notice about this person's physiology of confidence.

While the physiology of an emotion will be unique to each person, certain aspects usually show up across the board—for example, most happy people will smile or have an upward direction in their facial expressions, and depressed people usually have a sense of a downward direction in their faces and the energy of their bodies. But the real importance of discovering the physiology of an emotion is when you use it to access the emotion upon command. To access any emotion, look at your description of its physiology and copy that physiology exactly.

Here's an example of some common elements of the physiology of confidence, and some suggestions for intensifying that emotion within you.

The Physiology of Confidence

Posture: Strong and upright, with a slight lean forward.
Breathing: Relaxed. Deep breaths can intensify feeling.
Tension/Relaxation: A mixture of both. Tension produces a sense of energy, while relaxation shows the person is comfortable.
Gestures/Movement: Movement is strong, direct and powerful, and forward. Powerful movement intensifies feeling.
Facial Expression: Focused and relaxed. Usually a slight upward direction in the facial expression. A furrowed brow communicates intensity but not confidence.

Exercise

1. For each of the emotions in your OPI, use either of the methods described above to discover the physiology of that emotion. Write down the elements of each emotion.

_____

_____

_____

_____

2. Put yourself into that emotion's physiology, copying each element as exactly as you can.

3. Experiment with intensifying the emotion by changing the different aspects of posture, breath, movement, facial expression, tension and relaxation.

Your physiology immediately prior to and during your presentation will have a profound effect on your performance. I suggest you develop a *pre-presentation routine* where you put yourself into the physiology of each of your OPI emotions. In the beginning this will take some time and it should be something you do at home where you can get fully into those states. But every time you put yourself into the physiology of a particular emotion, you're building a trigger that will allow you to access that emotion more quickly.

Eventually, all you'll need to do is to stand in the way your body has come to associate to the emotion of confidence, and you'll feel confident. A friend of mine has rehearsed the emotion of confidence so many times that the moment she puts her shoulders back, breathes deeply, and puts a smile on her face, she automatically becomes confident. If you put in the "rehearsal" time for your OPI emotions while you're at home, you'll find those emotions will be at your fingertips when you do a presentation. (There's also a way to access those emotions right before you get up in front of your audience. You'll read more about your pre-presentation routine in Chapter 7.)

Trigger #2: Language and Submodalities

We all talk to ourselves all the time. Sometimes what we say is innocuous, sometimes it's great—and then there are the times that we use our inner self-talk to beat ourselves up. The negative language we use in our own heads can have a devastating effect on our effectiveness as a presenter. Why? Because *language is the way we define and describe everything.* And the words we use have a direct effect on what things mean to us and how we feel.

Let's take a concrete example. Your boss, Ron, comes into the office you share with Sue, John, and Mary, and uses a loud voice to express his opinion. After Ron leaves, Sue says, "Boy, he was forceful, wasn't he?" "Forceful!" John replies. "He was furious. I've never seen someone so angry." Mary adds, "He seemed kind of crazy to me. I hope he doesn't go postal and come back with a gun." But when you talk to Ron about it later, he tells you, "No, I wasn't angry—I just wanted to make sure everyone in the room could hear me." Each person saw the exact same thing, yet the words they use to describe the incident are completely different. And do you think each of your co-workers had a different experience of the incident? You bet.

Now let's apply this to your own internal experience. Imagine you're getting ready to give the most important presentation of your life. There's an audience of a thousand people waiting to hear you. If you do well, your future is assured. If you blow it, you'll never get a chance like this again. You're standing outside the room, your mind going a mile a minute. What kinds of things would you be saying to yourself? If you're saying, "Oh lord, please don't let me screw up," or asking yourself, "What if I fail?" or telling yourself, "I'm terrified—I can't do this," how well do you think you'll do? On the other hand, if you're saying things like, "What a great opportunity!" or "I'm so excited about helping these people solve their problems," or "No guts, no glory," or "Let me at 'em!" what kind of emotional state will you be in when you enter the room? And which kind of self-talk will create a better emotional state-the first or the second? Can you see why the language we use inside our own minds is so important when it comes to our emotions and the power of our presentations? *What you say to yourself determines what you focus on and how you feel.*

In working with presenters, I've noticed the language of those who struggle is very different from that of people who enjoy presenting. People who struggle tell me they are saying to themselves, "What if I screw this up?" "Why am I nervous?" and "Why is this so hard?" I tell them, "The first thing we have to do is to change what you're saying to yourself, because with that kind of self-talk you're going to be fighting an uphill battle."

Luckily, changing your self-talk is easy. Just as with physiology, the first step is to become aware of your own patterns—in this case, what you say to yourself on a regular basis. This is sometimes difficult, because we're all so used to our inner dialogue that we're hardly aware of it. You can start by noticing if there are any words or expressions you use regularly when it comes to speaking. Imagine that someone has just asked you to do a presentation in about an hour. What's the first thing that comes into your mind? The words and expressions you have linked to speaking may make you more excited or scared, resourceful or unresourceful, depending on what they are. Your job will be to get rid of any words and expressions that get in the way of your giving the best presentation possible, and create an entire "language list" of words and expressions that help you get into your best, most powerful emotional and physical states for every presentation.

There are several different types of language patterns that the brain uses to shape our perception of the world. Two key patterns are *questions* and *incantations*.

Questions

We are constantly asking questions in our mind—about what things are, what they mean, what we need to do, how we should do things, etc. The human brain is automatically wired to want to answer a question. That's why questions are such a powerful form of language, because *they can be used to direct the focus of our thoughts and emotions*. If you ask, "What if I screw up?" you'll focus on something different than if you asked, "How great will I be at this?" Questions also help us access emotions. If you want to feel happier, ask yourself questions like, "What should I be happy about in this situation?" If you want more confidence, questions like, "What do I already know that will help me here?" or "When have I been successful before?" will help. *The brain will do its best to answer every question you ask it.* Your job is to ask the best questions possible, so you will get high-quality answers that lead you to the state of being a persuasive presenter.

Questions can be divided into two categories: great questions and lousy questions. Great questions lead you into powerful and resourceful emotions and physiologies; lousy questions stop you in your tracks and make you feel completely unresourceful and defeated. These two kinds of questions also can be called *empowering* and *disempowering*. Examples of disempowering questions for a presenter include:

- Am I really ready to give this presentation?
- What if I screw this up?
- Why am I feeling so nervous?
- Does my audience like me?
- Why aren't they responding to me?

These questions create emotions like doubt, uncertainty, unresourcefulness, and fear. If you asked these questions either before or during a presentation, how do you think you would do? But what if you asked yourself empowering questions instead? Questions like . . .

- What's my outcome?
- What can I focus on now to be even more committed to my outcome?
- How can I have even more fun doing this presentation?
- How can I help my audience understand this even better?
- How can I put even more of myself into this presentation?

- How can I empower this audience to move toward our outcome?

To keep your brain focused on achieving the outcome for your presentation, any question that does not support you in achieving the outcome must be eliminated and replaced with an empowering question.

Exercise

1. Think about doing a presentation for an important audience. What questions do you find yourself asking inside your own mind? Write down all the questions you ask.

_____

_____

_____

_____

_____

_____

2. Take a look at your questions and categorize each one as empowering or disempowering. Keep the empowering ones. We'll learn how to eliminate the disempowering ones later in this chapter.

_____

_____

_____

_____

You also can use questions to help you access and intensify your OPI emotions. If you want to feel connected and caring, for instance, ask questions like, "What's great about this audience?" "How will what I have to offer these people change their lives and make them better?" "What do I know about this group that will connect me to them at an even deeper level?" If you want to access confidence, use questions like, "How great will this be?" "How lucky is this audience to hear me speak?" or "What do I know that will absolutely make a difference to this audience?" Most people need only three or four questions to get themselves into a particular emotional state. And like the triggers for physiology, the more you ask yourself these empowering questions, the easier it will be for you to access these great emotional states anytime you want.

Exercise

1. For each of the emotions you need to be in your OPI, come up with at least three to four questions that lead you into that emotion. Sometimes the easiest way to discover these questions is to put yourself into the physiology of the emotion, and in that state, see what questions come to your mind. Remember, physiology, language and submodalities, and beliefs are triggers, and any one or combination of them can cause you to experience a particular emotion at any given time.

2. Next, take a look at your OPI, your optimal performance
    identity, and come up with three or four questions that
    help you get into that state. Write these questions down,
    and use them whenever you are getting ready to do a
    presentation.

_____

_____

_____

_____

_____

_____

_____

Incantations

Most of us have heard of the word "incantation" in connection
with a magical formula of some kind. An incantation is also a magical
formula for a presenter, but the magic it creates is in our emotions.
For our purposes, an incantation is a *word or phrase repeated in
conjunction with a powerful physiology*. Like questions,
incantations direct our focus and trigger emotions. In fact, incantations
can be stronger than questions because they combine words and
physiology into one stimulus. They're some of our best tools when
it comes to creating and accessing our OPI.

Anyone who is afraid of public speaking has a phrase they
associate to the act of presenting that causes the emotion of fear to
be triggered. Here are some examples of disempowering incantations:

- Oh %&#!
- I hate this!
- This stinks!
- I stink at this!

- I can't!
- I feel terrible!
- I'm not ready yet!

Such words, when associated to a physiology of doubt and fear, will trigger unresourceful emotions that will stop you from ever doing a great job as a presenter. To change your results, you must change your emotions; to change your emotions, you must change the words you say to yourself. You need to start using incantations that give you a different picture of what is going to transpire when you present.

You must make sure that you are using empowering incantations before and during your presentation. Here are some empowering incantations you might like to adopt:

- I love this!
- This is awesome!
- Use everything!
- Yes!
- Let's go!

These incantations are short and easy to remember. They also trigger emotions of excitement and enthusiasm. I also use "Give it everything you've got" and "This is awesome." I say both incantations to myself every time I'm getting ready to present. These words have been linked to my OPI emotions, so whenever I say them I feel the emotions, and whenever I feel the emotions these words come to mind.

Your incantations can be anything that puts you into the powerful physiologies of your OPI emotions. You can use a favorite phrase from the military, for example, or an old school fight cheer—any short sentence or phrase that triggers powerful, positive emotions within you. When you say that phrase over and over while you put yourself into your OPI physiology, you're setting up a positive "feedback loop" within your body and mind. The phrase will trigger the emotion, which will then trigger the physiology. Or the physiology will trigger the emotion, which will then trigger your brain to repeat the incantation. Or the emotion will trigger the incantation, which will then trigger the physiology. Any element in the loop will cause the other two elements to be activated, and you'll have almost instant access to the powerful emotions you need to be a persuasive presenter.

Exercise

1. Looking at your OPI, come up with specific incantations that will trigger the physiology and emotions you will need. What are at least four incantations you can use to enable you to add value and achieve your outcome whenever you present? Make sure the incantations are short and easy to remember and they create positive emotions within you. Write these incantations down and repeat them to yourself while you are in those powerful emotions of your OPI.

_____

_____

_____

_____

2. As you think about presenting, notice if you have any disempowering incantations you need to eliminate for you to be the best presenter you can be. We'll talk about getting rid of those incantations later in this chapter.

_____

_____

_____

Submodalities

Now you're going to learn some of the finer points of using your mind to help you be a better presenter. You'll also learn a set of tools for changing any painful experience and making it feel better. Let's start by doing something we all do—use our imaginations. Imagine you are standing in front of a group getting ready to do a great presentation. Close your eyes and see the picture of that situation in your mind. (If you can't make a picture of it, imagine yourself watching it on TV.) What does the picture look like? Is it in black and white, or in color? Can you see yourself in the picture, or is it as if you were looking that the scene through your own eyes? Is the picture sharp and clear, or dim and fuzzy? Is it moving or still?

Now, notice if you can hear anything you're saying, or if you're talking to yourself about the presentation. What did you say? How did your voice sound? Was it loud or soft? Clear or muddled? Low or high? How fast or slow were you speaking?

Finally, check to see if there are any sensations in your body associated with this picture of standing in front of a group to present. Do you feel hot or cold? Energized or depressed? Is there movement? If so, is the movement fast or slow?

All of these questions have to do with what we call *submodalities*. Submodalities are the detailed ways our brains describe information we take in from the outside world. But what we're truly describing is our *internal* representation of the world outside us. We see something with our eyes, but we actually "see" the image inside the brain—the brain takes all the different bits of visual data fed to it by the eyes and then organizes the bits into something we recognize as a chair, or a car, or the face of someone we love. We think we are experiencing the world outside us, but in fact what we are really experiencing is our brain's interpretation of everything we take in from the world outside ourselves.

This fact, which has been proven through extensive research by neurobiologists and psychologists, works in our favor. It means that w*e have the power literally to change the way we experience an event, simply by changing the way our brain interprets it.* And to do that we can make use of the powerful tool of submodalities. Submodalities describe what we see, hear, or feel in very detailed precise ways. Every external and internal experience has submodalities associated to it. If you see something and describe your visual experience of it (not the parts of the picture itself but the characteristics of the picture), you will use submodalities like "clear," "bright," "dim," "color," "close," "far," and so on. If you hear something or say something to yourself, the sound or voice will have submodalities like "loud," "soft," "fast," "high," "grating," or whatever describes your own particular experience. If you feel something—an experience like walking outside on a very cold, windy day—you would use submodalities like "cold," "moving briskly," "pressure from the wind," etc.

There are specific submodalities in each of the three categories: visual (the characteristics of pictures), auditory (the characteristics of sounds), and kinesthetic (the characteristics of sensations). Here are some of them.

Visual submodalities
(It may help you to think of these as describing a picture on a TV screen.)
- Color or black and white
- Brightness
- Size of picture
- Size of central objects
- Distance of picture from you
- Distance of central object from you
- 3-D quality
- Intensity of color
- Degree of contrast
- Movement (speed, direction)
- Self in or out of picture

- Focus (where does your attention go in the picture?)
- Angle viewed from (in front? behind? to the side?)
- Number of pictures
- Still frame/motion picture

Auditory submodalities
- Volume
- Cadence
- Rhythm
- Inflections
- Tempo
- Pauses
- Tonality
- Timbre (the quality of the sound: sweet, deep, full, thin, etc.)
- Uniqueness of sound
- Location
- Direction
- Duration

Kinesthetic submodalities
- Temperature
- Texture
- Vibration
- Pressure
- Movement
- Duration
- Steady/intermittent
- Intensity
- Size
- Shape
- Weight
- Internal/external (is the experience inside your body or pressing on you from the outside)

There are two important keys to using submodalities. First, since submodalities are descriptions of our internal experience of the world, w*e can change the submodalities of any experience simply by telling our brains to do so.* And if we change the submodalities, how we feel about the experience often will change as well. Why? Because *submodalities describe our experience of any emotion.* Remember when we were talking about the feeling of happiness? Associated with that feeling you'll often find submodalities like "lightness," "energy," "upward movement," "quick tempo," and so on, whereas sadness will produce submodalities like "heaviness," "slow," "lack of energy," "downward movement," etc. Submodalities heavily influence our experience of any emotion. This means we can use submodalities to feel even better about the things we like, and to stop feeling so lousy about the things we don't!

Let's test this. Picture something you're afraid of. If it's public speaking, make a picture of yourself in front of a group that would make you very nervous. Describe the picture in terms of the list of visual submodalities on the previous page. (I suggest you write your description down.)

Now, here's the fun part. Take any one of those visual submodalities and change it. If the picture is bright, make it dim. If the picture is close to you, move it farther away. If it's sharp and clear, make the picture fuzzy. If it's in color, make it black and white. If there's movement, slow the movement down or stop it altogether. Change just one submodality and notice the effect on your emotions. Are you less nervous, more nervous, or about the same? There should be one or two submodalities that will increase or decrease your fear. (For most people making the picture dim, fuzzy, and farther away will decrease their nervousness. However, you may be different. Experiment with your picture and see what changes lessen your nervousness.)

You can do exactly the same thing with auditory and kinesthetic submodalities. If you have a boss whose voice drives you crazy, for instance, you can change the submodalities of his/her voice inside your own head. Speed it up so it sounds like Mickey Mouse. Make it sound sexy. Slow it down so you can barely understand the words. When you change the way the voice sounds, you will feel differently about it. With kinesthetic submodalities, let's say when you get up to do a presentation you start to feel butterflies in your stomach and you feel a sensation of heat in your hands and face. You could change this by slowing the butterflies down and letting them glide instead of fluttering, and then feel them alight gently inside you. Then you could imagine a gentle, cool rain falling on your face while you bathed your hands in the cool, fresh water of a babbling brook. By changing the submodalities of movement and heat, the feelings you associate with nervousness would disappear and the emotion would diminish as a result.

The second important thing about submodalities is that *certain submodalities will have more impact on our internal experience than others.* If you're feeling depressed, simply looking up instead of down often will help you feel better.

For example, if you have a fear of public speaking, you can lessen that fear simply by making a few minor adjustments to the submodalities of the pictures, sounds, and feelings you have.

Exercise

1. Take one presentation situation where you might experience a disempowering emotion—nervousness, fear, stuck, boredom, frustration, whatever the emotion might be for you.

_____

_____

_____

_____

_____

2. Identify the visual, auditory, and kinesthetic submodalities of that particular situation and write them down.

_____

_____

_____

_____

_____

_____

_____

3. Change the visual, auditory, and kinesthetic submodalities in turn, and notice the effect on the disempowering emotion. Is it lessened or increased?

4. Keep changing the visual, auditory, and kinesthetic submodalities until the disempowering emotion is completely gone.

You also can use submodalities to strengthen or enhance positive emotions. Think about a situation where you felt absolutely great-strong, certain, happy. Write down the visual, auditory, and kinesthetic submodalities of that experience. Now, take the different submodalities and change them so you feel even better. If the picture is bright, make it brighter. If it's at a medium distance, bring it closer. If it's still, make it a movie. Raise or lower the volume on the sound level, or bring the sound closer to you. (Think of the difference between someone saying, "I love you," from five feet away, and that same person whispering it in your ear.) Make yourself feel lighter, or more energetic and forceful, or faster or slower-whatever makes the experience even better.

Submodalities can be your greatest ally when it comes to creating the empowering emotions of your OPI. Why? There are very specific submodalities associated with each emotion, and you only need to discover those submodalities to be able to access that emotion upon command. And once you know the submodalities, you can change and/or enhance them so you can feel even more of that emotion at any time.

Exercise

1. For each of your OPI emotions, come up with at least one submodality for each category below that would help you create your OPI state. I've given you an example of one of my OPI emotions: confidence.
   - *Visual (Picture):* Clear, bright, focused, in color. I'm in the picture—I can see myself standing in front of the group.
   - *Auditory (Sound/music):* I say to myself, "Time to break through!" in a full, strong voice at a moderate tempo. I also hear the music, "We are the Champions" in the background.
   - *Kinesthetic (Sense of touch/feeling):* I'm moving with strength and authority. I feel strong in my body yet relaxed. The tempo of my movements is moderate but with a sense of direction and focused energy.

2. Experiment with changing or increasing the submodalities in each category to see if you can make the emotion even stronger.

When I first began presenting, I spent a lot of preparation time creating a picture in my mind what the ideal presentation would look, sound, and feel like. I adjusted the submodalities so the experience was the best I could imagine. My pictures were clear, sharp, full of color, very close to me but still far enough away that I could take in the entire room. I could hear my own voice sounding strong but not strident, with a comfortable pitch and lots of variation of tone and tempo. (I also could hear the thunderous applause from my audience when I finished!) I felt myself moving with strength and certainty, but with a sense of lightness and balance and comfort. I had enormous energy but also great relaxation. My movements weren't hurried but they were specific and clean.

I also used a metaphor to make my pictures even better. Metaphors are another way of describing our experience—like "breaking through a brick wall," "seeing the light," "stepping through the doorway," and so on.

I imagined my audience was trapped in darkness and the outcome of my presentation was a big, beautiful, bright light. I knew my presentation would help them to break through and see the light. I pictured that as I came onstage the audience and I were breaking through so we would see the light together. I rehearsed the picture of my ideal presentation over and over. And by the time I actually stood up in front of the group, I knew exactly what I wanted to do and how I would do it. And guess what? My picture matched the reality!

You, too, can create a picture in your mind that can motivate you in many different circumstances and situations. By creating your ideal picture and pairing it with a powerful metaphor, you'll find that you'll be unstoppable when you're called upon to present.

Exercise

1. What could you focus on using your visual, auditory, and
    kinesthetic submodalities that would inspire you to give an
    outstanding presentation? Create that scenario now. Then
    work with your submodalities to intensify it and make it even
    more powerful.

2. Is there a metaphor you could use that would get you
    excited about doing your presentation? Come up with a
    metaphor and make a picture of what that would look
    like for you.

Submodalities are useful in one final situation: to eliminate not just disempowering emotions but also patterns of physiology, language, and beliefs. At the end of this chapter you'll discover how you can do just that.

Emotional Trigger #3: Beliefs

The third trigger for our emotions is belief. A belief is a feeling of certainty about something. You believe the sun will come up tomorrow. You believe you are a man or a woman. You believe you live in a particular town or country. All of these are fairly self-evident and innocuous beliefs. But what about other beliefs we may hold about ourselves and our abilities? Have you ever heard someone say, "Oh, I'm not any good at _____ " (filling in the blank with things like math, spelling, driving, organizing, relationships)? Or they say things like, "I'm disadvantaged," or "I'm slow," or "I can't remember anything complicated?" Have you heard someone state, "That's just not who I am?" Or maybe you've said things like that yourself?

The problem is that such statements may or may not be true, but because we feel certain about them we don't even notice the times when they're not true. I've had friends tell me they're no good at math, but they can figure out baseball statistics in their heads. I've known other people who tell me they're terrified of public speaking, yet they happily perform in their church choir or speak in front of their children's Scout troupe. And I know a woman who refuses to have anything to do with her car because it's "too complicated," yet she can figure out exactly what's wrong with the database at work even when no one else can!

Human beings will do whatever it takes to be consistent with their beliefs. When we have a belief about something, our brains will delete any contrary examples that may occur, simply because we can't stand the inner conflict. This is especially true about beliefs about who we are—our *identity*. Identity beliefs often include the words "I am." Beware using the words "I am," and following them with any kind of negative quality or statement of fact! "I am" means we regard what follows as part of our make-up, and we will feel threatened whenever anything occurs that shows us that belief is untrue, even if the belief is destructive.

Whenever I work with people on their presentation skills, the first thing I do is to ask them, "What are your beliefs about presenting?" I do this because I know how disempowering beliefs can cause people to sabotage themselves. I can train someone in all the best skills; I can show them my entire FIRE-UP! System; they can have the best content in the world; but if they don't believe they can do a good job, they won't.

One of the keys to becoming a great presenter is to discover any disempowering beliefs you may have about presenting.

Here are some typical examples:

- I'm not the best presenter on this topic.
- I don't know my content that well.
- This audience is really tough.
- Our solution is going to be too expensive for this customer.
- Another company has a product with features that ours doesn't have.
- I don't enjoy speaking.
- I'm afraid.
- I can't talk to this many people (or this powerful a group) without messing up.

Exercise

Think about giving a presentation. Notice if you have any disempowering beliefs you need to eliminate for you to be the best presenter possible. Write those beliefs down—we'll get rid of them later.

Fortunately, we also can have very positive and empowering beliefs about ourselves and our abilities. "I'm a great presenter" is an example of an empowering identity belief. "I can do almost anything as long as I commit enough time and focus to mastering it" is an example of another empowering belief. "I succeed every time I give it my best" is another great belief to adopt.

Here are some examples of empowering beliefs when it comes to being a persuasive presenter:

- I am the best presenter in the world on this topic for this group at this time.
- I am a master of my content for this presentation.
- This is an awesome audience!
- Our total solution is an incredible value for this customer.
- Our overall solution is far superior to anything our competitors can offer.
- This audience needs what we have to offer, and I'm ready to show them how.
- No matter what happens, this audience will receive enormous value from our time together.
- I get better each and every time I'm in front of a group.

Exercise

What are the empowering beliefs you must have in order to become a persuasive presenter? Come up with a list of at least five to ten great beliefs and write them down. Make sure some of them are identity beliefs (use the words "I am") and some are beliefs about your audience and your outcome.

_____

_____

_____

_____

_____

_____

_____

_____

_____

_____

Installing new beliefs is very easy. First, *come up with at least five reasons each belief is true.* Use references from your past if you can. When were you a great presenter? Why should you care about this audience? What's great about your product or topic that this audience needs to know?

Then you can *use the other emotional triggers to help you install your new empowering beliefs.* After all, what is a belief? It's made up of words, or language. And a belief is a feeling of being certain about something, and certainty is an emotion that has a particular pattern of physiology. So if you get yourself into a physiology of certainty and then say the belief again and again, you'll associate the words to the physiology. You'll also be turning the belief into an incantation. You see how neatly the three emotional triggers work in unison to help you prepare yourself mentally and emotionally to be at your best?

In the same way, once you build a good, solid, empowering belief, you can then use the belief to help you access the physiology of your OPI on command. I've repeated my empowering beliefs so many times that all I have to do is say, "I am the best presenter in the world on this topic for this group at this time," and I feel a rush of confidence, excitement, commitment, and a sense of adventure and daring. You can do the same with your own empowering beliefs. The more you say them while you're in your OPI emotions and physiology, the easier it will be for you to believe what you say, and to feel those emotions while you say them.

Exercise

1. Take a look at the empowering beliefs you wrote earlier, and next to each belief write at least five reasons why this belief is true. For instance, for the belief, "I'm the best presenter in the world on this topic, for this group at this time," I wrote, "This is true because I'm the one that's here! This is true because I know this group's needs, wants, and problems, and I've got an elegant solution that will make their lives better."

_____

_____

_____

_____

_____

_____

_____

_____

_____

2. Look at each of your OPI emotions and come up with an empowering belief that will help you access that emotion easily. Follow each belief with five reasons that it is true. For example, by "adventurous and daring," I wrote, "I love doing something new and different and learning as a result." The reason this is true is, "Every time I've tried something new I learned so much that I got far more than if I had done things the same old way."

_____

_____

_____

_____

_____

_____

_____

_____

_____

As you continue to work on your presentations, notice the beliefs that crop up. Anything that you're certain about is in reality nothing more than a belief. Some beliefs are very useful, like the belief you'll wake up tomorrow morning! But most beliefs will benefit from a little judicious examination.

Take a look at your beliefs and see if they are empowering or disempowering. Then turn the empowering ones into an incantation by associating them to powerful physiologies. And if you need to get rid of any disempowering ones, that's what we will do next.

Getting Rid of Disempowering Patterns of Physiology, Language, and Beliefs

You're about to learn how easy it is to get rid of any pattern of physiology, language, and belief that may be holding you back from being the best presenter you can be. You'll actually be using a tool we've already discussed: submodalities. And you're going to love how easy it is to change even the most ingrained patterns in a matter of a few minutes.

As you learned earlier, every single internal experience is made up of visual, auditory, and kinesthetic submodalities. By changing the submodalities of the internal experience, you can literally change the experience itself. Think of someone you really don't like, and make a picture of his or her face in your mind. Now move that picture away from you until it's just a tiny dot in the distance. Is the experience of that person less intense when they are far away? Imagine someone yelling at you, and then turn the volume way down. Do you have a different reaction? Think of someone coming up and hitting you hard on the head. Now, have the same thing happen, only this time they tap you lightly. A different experience, right?

When it comes to disempowering patterns of physiology, language, and belief, we're going to take this a few steps further. We're not just going to lessen the severity of these patterns; we're going to scramble them so you will have difficulty ever accessing them again! It's just like scrambling an egg—no matter how hard you try, you can't unscramble an egg once you've broken it and whipped it up.

The scramble is one of the fundamental tools of NLP, and it's an incredibly effective one. In order for this to work, however, you have to be willing to be completely silly and stupid and outrageous. The more outrageous you are, the more effective the scramble will be and the longer lasting its results. I'm going to give you three specific examples of scrambling a visual pattern, a physiological pattern and a language pattern (a belief).

Scrambling a Visual Pattern

Sometimes people are triggered to go into disempowered emotions when they see a certain person or they're put into a certain situation. Let's take a common problem for presenters: being in front of a large audience.

1. Imagine yourself in front of a very large audience, one that creates disempowering emotions for you. ("Large" can be five, fifty, five hundred, five thousand, or fifty thousand people.) Or perhaps you would feel unable to handle an important audience, like the president of the United States, your spouse, your boss, or your parents. Come up with a situation in which you would feel uncomfortable presenting.

_____

_____

_____

_____

_____

_____

_____

_____

2. As you look out at that audience, notice what the picture is like. Use the list of visual submodalities on page XX to describe the picture. Is it close or far away? Bright or dim? Clear or fuzzy? A movie or a still picture? Color or black and white? Are you in the picture or not? What angle are you viewing this picture from? Take notes of every aspect of this picture.

3. As you keep looking at the picture, change each visual submodality in turn and notice what effect if any it has on your emotional state. If this picture is close, move it farther away. If it's bright, dim it. If it's dim, make it brighter. If it's a movie, make it a still picture. If it's black and white, make it color. Some of these changes may make your disempowering emotion stronger. If so, change it back the way it was. But some of these changes will undoubtedly make the feeling less.

4. Now it's time to have some fun! As you look at this audience, do something to make them ridiculous. See them in their underwear. Put clown wigs and makeup on them. Give them funny ears. Have them smile at you as if you were their best friend. See them cheering you madly. Notice what effect any or all of these changes have on your emotions. If you're like most people, you'll feel better immediately.

5. Now turn the picture into your favorite cartoon. Watch your audience become cartoon characters, and see them running around like lunatics, doing what cartoon characters do. If you want, put silly cartoon music with the scene.

6. For the last step, speed the cartoon up double and triple time. See everyone running around like crazy people at hyper speed. Now run the cartoon backwards, then forwards, then backwards, again and again. Hear the cartoon music speeding up and running backwards, too.

7. Take a look at the audience sitting there, and see if you feel differently about presenting to them. They probably are a lot less intimidating!

Scrambling a Pattern of Physiology

This scramble is very useful if you feel fear when you get up to speak, but you can use it for any disempowering emotion.

1. Think of a time when you felt this fear. Using the list of kinesthetic submodalities on page XX, describe the physical elements of this pattern. For example, "As I'm moving toward the room I get this feeling of pressure in my stomach, like I'm going to throw up. My hands get cold and my face gets hot. I feel like all the energy is draining from my body. I take one step toward the room and the feelings intensify. My eyes start to water. I feel myself leaning backward, I shake my head and wave my hands, and then I turn and walk away as fast as I can." Write down your own specific pattern.

_____

_____

_____

_____

_____

_____

_____

2. Imagine yourself moving backwards in time to the point right before you started feeling fear. Feel all your emotions and sensations literally running backwards until you feel normal. Now, run the pattern forward again, only run it triple time, as if you were a cartoon character (sound familiar?). Run toward the room, waving your arms, shaking your head, then turn around and walking away at hyper-speed. Then run the entire scene

backwards—feel yourself waving your hands backwards, shaking your head in the opposite direction, leaning forward, then taking a step back, then more steps, then more steps. You can make funny sounds while you do this, too. Run it backwards and forwards triple time until it becomes a blur.

3. Now, run the entire pattern at extremely slow speed, as if you were caught in a space warp where you could only move a few inches at a time. Make sounds at slow speed, too. Do this forward and backward at least twice.

4. Taking a look at the description of your old kinesthetic submodalities, change each one in turn and notice what effect (if any) it has on your emotional state. Instead of pressure in your stomach, feel a sensation of calm.

    Feel like your hands are encased in soft, warm gloves. Feel your face getting cooler, like someone put a cool washcloth on your forehead and cheeks. Imagine there is someone pouring energy into your body, filling you up with balanced, light, clear energy. Take a step toward the room, and feel all of these positive submodalities increase—you feel better with every step! Put a smile on your face and enjoy how great you feel.

Scrambling a Pattern of Language/Beliefs
I've saved language and beliefs for last because it's the most fun scramble of all.

*   Take the disempowering language pattern and/or belief you want to scramble. For example, "I'm not a great presenter."

- Say this statement to yourself, using the tone of voice that you typically use. Describe what it sounds like using the list of auditory submodalities. For example, "My voice is low, without much volume, I'm speaking at a slow speed, I emphasize the word 'not,' I kind of sigh when I say it." Write your list down.

- Next, say this statement like Mickey Mouse would say it-fast, high, cartoon-y. Repeat it for at least a minute. Put a big smile on your face while you say it.

- Say it in a sexy voice, as if you were whispering it in someone's ear. Say it this way for a minute, and enjoy it!

- Sing it like it's a line from a country Western song, or an opera. Act like you're that kind of performer, too.

- Do the opposite of the auditory submodalities you listed earlier. Shout it at the top of your lungs, speed it up, emphasize all kinds of different words, say it on one breath until you run out of air.

- Say the statement backwards, faster and faster. If you really want to scramble the pattern, add physiology: turn in circles while you say it. Stick your finger up your nose while you say it. Hop on one foot while you say it. Do it with a big grin on your face while you say it.

- Now, think of the statement, "I'm not a great presenter." It's pretty silly, isn't it?

With all these scrambles, you want to make sure that you create something new and empowering to take the place of the old pattern. Come up with new patterns of physiology, language, and/or beliefs that will help you attain and sustain your optimal performance identity. This is a vital part of your preparation for being a persuasive presenter. You'll also have a great time creating some powerful new emotions, physiologies, language and beliefs that will support you in every part of your life!

Chapter 6 Highlights

Phase Two of preparation is getting yourself into the right mental and emotional state. You start by defining your Optimal Performance Identity (OPI). To create your OPI, think about a great presentation you did, and describe your emotions and outcomes.

You also must define the emotions you must feel in order to perform at your peak. Ask, "What emotions will I need to access to accomplish the outcomes in my OPI? Are there any emotions that I must get rid of?"

You access your OPI emotions by discovering the unique mental and physical formula for each one. You can utilize the *Three Emotional Triggers*, factors that will allow you to trigger each emotion immediately.

1. **Physiology**: posture, breathing, gestures and movement, facial expressions, and muscle tension or relaxation. You can access the physiology of a particular emotion by (1) remembering a time when you felt that emotion, and putting your body and mind back into that moment; (2) thinking of someone who you believe epitomizes that emotion, and copy his or her physiology exactly.

2. **Language and Submodalities**. Language is the way you define and describe everything. What you say to yourself determines what you focus on and how you feel. Two key language patterns are *questions* and *incantations.*

   • Questions direct the focus of our thoughts and emotions. Questions can be either empowering or disempowering. Any disempowering questions should be eliminated and replaced with empowering ones.

- An incantation is a word or phrase repeated in conjunction with a powerful physiology. Make sure that you are using empowering incantations before and during presentations.

- Submodalities are the detailed ways our brains describe our internal representation of the world— what we see, hear, or feel (visual, auditory, and kinesthetic). Submodalities also describe our experience of an emotion. We can change the way we experience an event or how we feel about it by changing the submodalities.

3. **Beliefs**. A belief is a feeling of certainty about something. Identity beliefs—beliefs about who we are—are especially powerful. To be a great presenter, you must eliminate any disempowering beliefs about yourself and presenting, and install empowering ones.

It's easy to get rid of any pattern of physiology, language, and belief that may be holding you back by using a scramble pattern. We can scramble visual patterns, patterns of physiology, and patterns of language and beliefs.

Chapter Seven
Presentation Day:
Your Checklist for Success

If you've done your preparation, the actual day of your presentation should be an event to look forward to. But there are a few more things you can do that day to ensure a successful outcome to your presentation as well as your enjoyment of the entire experience. Think of the day of a presentation like the day of a big race for a runner. Runners spend hours every week preparing themselves physically, mentally, and emotionally for competition. When the day of the race arrives, the runners are as ready as they can possibly make themselves. Yet if you watch the top runners, they all have different routines they follow to make sure that when the starting gun goes off, they'll be in top form. As a presenter you, too, can develop routines that will help you be your best when you're introduced to a group and it's your turn to "run."

Let's start with some suggestions for preparing yourself the night before.

The Night Before a Presentation
The day or night before any presentation, start by getting yourself into your OPI. Try the following routine.

- Review your OPI and say it to yourself several times, with feeling and positive emotion. Ask yourself, "How will I show up in this identity tomorrow during my presentation?" See yourself in front of your audience as this person.

- Review your OPI emotional recipe. Repeat your emotional OPI to yourself with passion, using "I am" statements: "I am caring," "I am powerful," "I am committed," whatever your OPI emotions are.

- Put yourself into each of your OPI emotions using the triggers of physiology, language and submodalities, and beliefs.

- Do a final check to see if there are any disempowering beliefs, language patterns, or feelings that you need to get rid of so you can be your best tomorrow. Use the scramble techniques described in the last chapter to eliminate them.

Getting into your OPI and your OPI emotions the night before a presentation guarantees that you will have easy access to them when you're in front of a group. And the more often you put yourself into these states, the easier it will be to access them even in stressful situations.

Once you've accessed the identity, emotions, and physiology of a great presenter, you're ready to focus on the specifics for this particular presentation.

- Review your outcome. Make sure it's absolutely clear in your mind, and that it's something you can completely support.

- Review what you know about your audience. Associate to anything you can truly like about this group.

- Visualize yourself achieving your outcome at the end of your presentation: you're getting the order, your audience is applauding you, you've created enormous value for the group, and so on.

- Review the "ladder rungs" of your content-each of the six steps of FIRE-UP! (We'll be going through these steps later.) Make sure that every aspect of your presentation contributes to the outcome.

- Review your presentation materials. Make sure you have all the audiovisual materials ready (with backups just in case), and that the materials are organized and easily accessible.

- Make sure your clothes for the next day are ready, too—you don't want any last-minute surprises caused by a suit not back from the cleaners or an unsuspected spot on the shirt you planned to wear.

Now you can go to sleep knowing that you have done everything you possibly can to be ready for your presentation. And a good night's sleep is also a great way to prepare to be at your best the next day.

Presentation Day: Before You Arrive

Just like an athlete on the day of a big race, setting up a morning routine helps ensure that you've taken care of everything.

- Get up early so you'll have plenty of time to get ready. There's nothing that will throw you off faster than rushing.

- Make sure your body is stretched out and relaxed. I recommend that speakers do some kind of mild exercise the morning of a presentation so they're feeling in great shape physically. Stretching, yoga, calisthenics, walking and jogging are all excellent. Whatever exercise you do, however, it should be something that energizes and relaxes rather than drains you.

- Some people like to eat very little before a presentation, while others like a hearty meal. Find out what works for you, and do that. But always make sure to drink lots of water the day of a presentation.

You want your mouth and throat well lubricated so you can avoid problems like coughing, clearing your throat, or losing your voice.

• Do one final check of all your presentation materials before you leave. Take with you copies of your outcome, your OPI, your OPI emotions, and any important information about the group the presentation is for.

• Leave early enough that you will arrive at least thirty minutes to an hour in advance. Why arrive so early? Because the next stage of your preparation occurs at the presentation location itself.

Presentation Day: At the Presentation Location

You've done a great job of preparing yourself, but now you must prepare the space. Sometimes you will have no control over the space in which you'll be doing a presentation, but other times you can adjust the space to make your job a lot easier.

In preparing the space, remember that *you own the room* because you own the outcome. You want to set things up to give you the greatest likelihood for success. Get to the meeting site early and walk around the room; this will help you make the space your own. Then put yourself in your audience's place. Try sitting in different places around the room and ask yourself, "When I'm sitting here, how do I feel? If I'm standing there, what am I going to look like to someone in this chair?" See if there are any changes you wish to make in the room's layout. Enlist the support of the person who brought you in for the presentation to get the changes made. Remember, your goal as a presenter is to connect with your audience, and the space can either help or hinder you in that task. Set up the space so you can connect as easily as possible with your audience.

Here are some key items to take into account when you are preparing the presentation room.

1. **Keep as much light in the room as possible.** Light keeps people more alert; if it gets too dark people tend to get groggy or go to sleep. If you're using audiovisual materials (like PowerPoint slides) that require a darkened room, see if you can lower the light in the end of the room where the materials will be shown while keeping the lights at a higher level everywhere else. If you have to lower the lights in the entire room, bring the lights down only during the time you are showing your audiovisual material, and then bring them back up as quickly as possible.

2. **Position your audience as close to you as possible.** Think about the difference between talking with a group of people gathered around a small table versus speaking to the same group while they are seated in the back of an auditorium. Which group will be easier to reach emotionally? When people are closer, you also don't have to work as hard to be heard or seen.

    *   If you're presenting in a conference room, make sure the chairs are positioned around the table so that it's easy for you to talk to people. If you're presenting from a stage, make sure the first row of chairs is close enough that you can see people comfortably. In most places the first row of chairs are twelve feet away from the front of the stage, and that gap can feel like a chasm when you're trying to communicate with your audience. Bring the first row of chairs as close as possible to the front of the stage to allow you to see your audience and them to see you without straining.

3. **If the chairs in the room are set up theatre style (in rows, with a "stage" area for the presenter in the front of the room), eliminate middle aisles whenever possible.** Why? As a presenter, you will be using the entire stage area (see Chapter 15), but you'll naturally spend most of your time in the middle. If you have an aisle right in front of you as you stand in the middle of the stage, all that great energy and passion and communication you're directing toward your audience will vanish. Instead, set the room up with side aisles and keep your audience in front of you.

The following diagram is ideal for setting up the chairs in your presentation space.

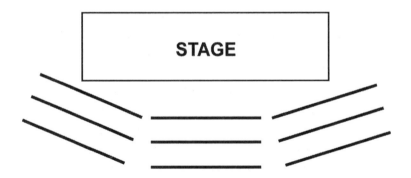

4. **If possible, find out how many people will be attending your presentation, and get rid of any extra chairs.** You want your audience seated in a group. Don't be afraid to move chairs or take them out of the room completely. It's better to add chairs later than to have to speak to people that are scattered around a room.

5. **Make sure your presentation space is big enough to let you connect with your entire audience.** If the space you've been given as your stage area is five feet

wide, for instance, and you have people seated twenty feet to either side of the stage, you're going to have to work very hard to talk to the people in the corners. Walk the space in which you're going to be presenting and check out the placement of your audience, and if you need to, ask for more room on the sides so you can walk over and talk to the people in the corners during your presentation.

6. **Take a look at the wall or space that will be behind you when you are presenting**. Is there anything that might draw the focus of your audience away from you— a light that will be shining in the audience's eyes, for instance, or a glass wall or window with people walking by outside of it? Make sure that there is nothing behind you that could distract your listeners. Ask for curtains to be drawn, the light to be turned off, and so on. If necessary, see if you can re-orient the presentation space so there is a neutral or blank wall behind you.

7. **Check and double-check all technical equipment** (microphones, computers, music, projectors, etc.) well before the time you are scheduled to speak. If you're working with someone as your audiovisual support, make sure they're absolutely clear about what you want done and when.

Your presentation space can either enhance or detract from the connection you establish with your audience. When you're not connected, it's like the physical, mental, and emotion fuel you created with your OPI is being spilled and wasted, falling to the floor rather than feeding the flame within each person.

By setting up your presentation space to enhance connection, you're making your job as a presenter far easier, and helping to create a better experience for you audience as well.

Your Pre-Presentation Routine

You've prepared the room, your audiovisual support materials are ready to go, it's about fifteen to twenty minutes before your presentation is scheduled to begin—now's the time to trigger the physical, mental, and emotional triggers that will help you get in your optimal performance state.

I suggest that most presenters go off by themselves for a few moments and do the following pre-speech routine.

- Read the outcome for your presentation again and get totally connected to it.

- Make sure your body is well stretched and relaxed. If you're feeling tension, do something to get rid of it. Tension in the body can create tension in the mind, and your words and ideas may not flow freely. Sometimes tension is almost subliminal—you're not even aware of it, but it can affect your whole presentation.

  To get rid of tension, do something big with your physiology to help you convert the tension into a more powerful emotion. Run around the room. Punch a curtain. Jump up and down. Making a big change in your physiology will help release excess energy and help you get to a "blank slate" physically.

- Go through each of your OPI emotions and make sure that you can trigger them using your physiology, language and submodalities, and beliefs.

- I also recommend that speakers do this "Presentation Emotional Checkup Exercise" as part of their preparation.

Exercise: Presentation Emotional Checkup

1. Ask yourself, "What emotions am I experiencing now?" Then ask, "What emotion could I create right now in order to be able to present more effectively?"

_____

_____

_____

_____

_____

_____

_____

_____

_____

_____

2. Use the three emotional triggers (physiology, language, submodalities, and beliefs) to create the new emotion.

_____

_____

_____

_____

_____

3. Reinforce and maintain the pattern of the new emotion as you get ready to present. I like to "overdo" my emotions as part of my preparation—take my emotions to level one hundred, for example. Then, when I need these emotions at level ten during my presentation, accessing them at that level is a piece of cake.

_____

_____

_____

_____

_____

_____

This pre-presentation routine should take you no more than about five minutes. Afterwards, you'll be ready to meet your audience for the very first time, knowing that all the emotions you will need to connect with them are at your fingertips, and having a clear picture of your outcome for the day.

Meeting Your Audience: The Secret of Great Connection

Here's the final secret for making your job as a presenter as easy as possible: the first time you meet your audience shouldn't be when you step onstage or in front of the group. The earlier you establish connection with your audience, the better. Here are a few ways you can connect with your audience before you start your presentation.

- Get there early and mingle with the group. This will help you to relax and feel more connected to people as individuals. In some situations you'll be making a grand entrance—someone will introduce you and you'll go onstage—but even in situations like that, I suggest you either stand in the back as your audience comes in or look at them from backstage. Get a sense of who they are and how they're feeling. You'll start to feel more connected with them before you ever say a word.

- As you look at your audience, see these people as friendly. See yourself on the same side as them. They're your partners, not your opponents. You're there to help them, and they'll be happy to hear what you have to say.

- Visualize your energy connecting with the audience. Give the audience a "virtual" handshake or a pat on the back before you begin speaking. Remember what you like (or could like) about these people.

- If you need to do so, get out of sight and use your triggers to get in your OPI emotions right before you start your presentation.

One final point: If at all possible, make sure you have someone introduce you, perhaps the person who's been serving as your contact. There are two advantages to having someone introduce you. First, this person can get the group settled down and ready to listen to you. Second, your introducer can say nice things about you that you could never get away with saying about yourself! Many speakers have a standard "bio" that they use as the basis for any introduction. I prefer to chat with the person who's going to introduce me and give them one or two important points that I like to have mentioned. Then I ask them to use their own words and to keep it brief.

It's time! You're absolutely ready to give your best and to put all your energy and focus into connecting with your audience and achieving the outcome you have created. Now we're going to look at how to achieve that outcome. To climb from the foundation you've created to reach the outcome you want, you need two more parts of the FIRE-UP ladder. You need to create the "rungs" of your content, of course. But equally important, you need to know what the sides of your ladder are-the values that will guide your content.

Chapter 7 Highlights

- The night before your presentation, review your optimal performance identity (OPI) and your OPI emotional recipe. Put yourself into your OPI states using physiology, language and submodalities, and beliefs. Check and scramble any disempowering states or beliefs. Review your outcome and visualize achieving it. Review what you know about your audience and what you like about them. Go over your content and your presentation materials. Get your clothes ready. Make sure everything is ready for the next day.

- The day of your presentation, allow plenty of time to get ready. Do some kind of mild exercise to prepare your body physically. Eat what will make you feel light and ready to go. Drink plenty of water. Check your materials, and leave so you can arrive at least thirty minutes in advance.

- At the location, walk around the room. Put yourself in your audience's place to make sure everyone can see and hear you. Make sure there's plenty of light, that your audience is seated close to you, and there is no middle aisle in the audience. Get rid of extra chairs. Double-check any technical equipment.

- Right before your presentation, read your outcome again, get rid of any tension in your body, and go through your OPI emotions.

- Take time to connect with your audience before the presentation. Get there early and mingle with the group. See the people as friendly and on your side. Remember what you like about your audience. If possible, have someone introduce you to the group.

Chapter Eight
Communicate With Integrity and Power:
The FIRE-UP Ladder to Success

Real power and persuasion always come from speaking with integrity. That means everything you say must align with your values—things like honesty, courage, compassion, and trust. Staying true to your values is always the best way to communicate with power, passion, and effectiveness.

The sides of the FIRE-UP ladder represent your values. They are the guides that hold the steps in place as you go from point A (the foundation of what we know about this audience) to point B (the outcome of the presentation—the action that we want the audience to take). When we stay within our values, we can climb the rungs of our content quickly and easily. If, however, we stray outside our values, then just like trying to step outside the ladder, we will rest our foot on thin air.

Some presenters come from the "Do as I say, not as I do" school of speaking. They deliver a great talk about the importance of teamwork, then they treat their own team members like dirt. They preach about business ethics yet are not above taking a few kickbacks themselves. But no matter how well such a presenter may "talk the talk," I believe the people in the audience will sense the fundamental difference between what's being said and who the presenter really is. As a presenter, you can't stand in front of an audience and lie to them and not have it come back to haunt you in the end.

Unfortunately, those of us who are in the business of persuasion are usually trained to use whatever it takes to get the sale—exaggerating what our product/service can do; spreading rumors about competitors; not mentioning certain facts if they will affect our ability to close the deal; even something as simple as trying to make ourselves sound more successful than we really are by embellishing a resume. But I believe that every step outside of our values is dangerous—not only because we can get caught in a lie, but also because of what these lies do to us inside.

You may be tempted to violate your values. If you give in to the temptation, you may make your point, but ultimately you will weaken yourself and your ability to communicate with integrity and power in the future. You've got to focus on being true to who you are and being honest, so that when you get up and talk people know you can be trusted. Staying true to your values is always the best way to communicate.

Exercise
1. Think about a situation in which someone giving a presentation did not have integrity. How did you feel about that person? Would you want to attend another presentation by him or her?

_____

_____

_____

_____

2. Think about a person who speaks from integrity and in alignment with his or her values. How do you feel about that person?

_____

_____

_____

_____

Everyone has values that are important to them, but as presenters I believe two specific values are essential for keeping the ladder of our presentation strong. The first is honesty/ truthfulness. Your audience has to feel that you will tell them the truth whether it's in your best interest or not. As a presenter, if you are ever caught in a lie, falsehood, or even an exaggeration, your authority with that audience goes right out the window, and it will be difficult to impossible to get their trust back again.

Remember the old story of the boy who cried wolf. When the townspeople found out the boy was lying about seeing a wolf, they stopped listening to him, even when the wolf really did appear. If you're caught in just one fib or exaggeration in an hour's truthful presentation, that one fib can cause your audience to discount everything else you've said.

To my mind, it's not worth the risk. Speaking (and living) by the value of honesty/truthfulness will give you a strong support and guide for the rungs (content) of your presentation.

The second essential value is *putting your audience and their success before your own.* As persuasive presenters, we absolutely want to reach our predetermined outcome (which, as you remember, we created to serve our audience's best interests). But how many times have you seen speakers or presenters who are so focused on making the sale that they seem to ignore the audience entirely? That's not the way to persuade others.

People need to feel you are on their side, that you are just as invested in them and their success as they are, and that your outcome is designed to solve their problems and make their lives better, not just to make the sale.

Focusing on your audience and their success will keep you out of the "I" trap (where every other word out of your mouth is "I") and help you gain the audience's trust. It also will help you stay out of your own head and keep focused on what's really important—what your audience is thinking and feeling (more about this in Chapter 9). Finally, it will help you stay in integrity with yourself and your highest values.

I call the values of honesty/truthfulness and putting your audience and their success first, the Power Zone Values. I have made them a part of the recipe for my OPI. Before every presentation I remind myself of these values using two statements that describe them for me. You're welcome to use these statements or to come up with definitions of your own.

> **HONESTY/TRUTHFULNESS:** People can count on me to tell the truth.
> **AUDIENCE/CUSTOMER SUCCESS:** My energy, attention, and focus are on my audience's needs and success throughout my presentation.

With these two values as the sides of your ladder, your integrity and congruency will shine throughout your presentation. And in truth, these values are natural parts of who you are when you are at your best. And isn't that who you want to be when you are speaking?

Let's review where we are in the FIRE-UP ladder of outstanding presentations. Here are the four components in both list and "ladder" form:

1. Focus on your outcome.
2. Prepare yourself.
3. Communicate with integrity and power.
4. FIRE-UP! your audience to achieve your outcome.

At this point you've created an outcome for your presentation, you've prepared yourself mentally and emotionally, and you're committed to presenting with integrity. You're ready to construct the rungs of your ladder—the six components of a persuasive presentation. Each rung is designed to take you and your audience from the foundation you've created, up a series of emotional and logical steps based on their wants, wounds, and needs, until you reach the outcome of a solution that will benefit both audience and presenter.

In the next section of this book we'll discuss each rung in turn. You'll discover why each rung is essential and why it must be in its own unique position. And you'll gain knowledge, strategies, and practical hints that will make using the "FIRE-UP!" system easy and effortless.

Chapter 8 Highlights

- Real power and persuasion come from speaking with integrity, in agreement and in alignment with your values, which form the sides of the FIRE-UP ladder.

- Two values are essential for keeping the ladder of our presentation strong: (1) honesty/truthfulness, and (2) putting your audience and their success before your own.

Chapter Nine
FIRE 'EM UP!
CLIMBING THE "FIRE-UP"
LADDER TO SUCCESS

Remember the scene in *Braveheart* that I mentioned earlier? The Scots are facing a better—equipped and far larger army of English soldiers and, quite frankly, they're scared. They don't see the value in laying down their lives in what looks like a losing cause. One old soldier tries to rally the troops to stay put so they can negotiate with the English from strength, but the Scots start to leave the battlefield—until William Wallace rides up. He tells the Scots that yes, the day looks desperate and yes, they may lose their lives in the battle. But he also tells them that if they stay and fight, they'll gain something far more precious than their lives: freedom for themselves and their country. Wallace fans the flame of the Scots' courage and pride, and the entire army charges across the field to fight-and defeat-the English.

Inside each person is a small, flickering flame of potential, and the job of a persuasive presenter is to make that flame a rip-roaring fire of massive action. *The fuel for that fire is your presentation.* That's why the content of your presentation is represented by the acronym "FIRE-UP."

The goal of every persuasive presentation is to fuel the fire of potential in the audience-by making them aware of their pain, wants, needs, and desires so they're eager to take action on the outcome you propose. You're not just speaking to get people interested, to entertain them, or to make them curious. You want to make the fire within them burn so brightly that they must take action.

But as many battlefield leaders have found to their dismay, persuading an army isn't as simple as standing in front of them and yelling, "Let's go!" Firing people up requires many different kinds of fuel. And that's why the "FIRE-UP" System provides six simple, clear steps to move your audience from where they are to where you wish them to be: *excited, motivated, and ready to act.*

The six steps are:
F = Focus your audience's attention on you and your message.
I = Inform your audience of your purpose.
R = Remind your audience of their pain.
E = Educate, empower, and entertain your audience.
U = Use your audience's uniqueness to demonstrate a solution to their problems.
P = Propose a commitment and close with emotion.

In the following chapters we'll go over each step in turn. You'll discover why each step is essential and why it must be in its own unique position. And you'll gain knowledge, strategies, and practical hints that will make you an expert at using the "FIRE-UP" System!

Chapter Ten
F = Focus Your Audience's Attention on You and Your Message

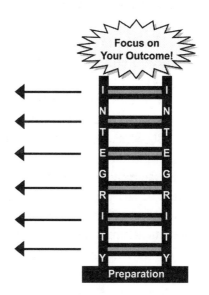

Focus on Your Outcome!

Propose a commitment and close with emotion

Use their uniqueness to demonstrate a solution

Educate, empower and entertain your audience

Remind your audience of their pain

Inform your audience of your purpose

Focus your audience's attention on you

INTEGRITY

Preparation

A few years ago I was asked to speak at a weekend conference for a large pharmaceutical company. The night before I was due to speak I got in late, so I went straight to bed and then got up early in the morning to mingle with people at breakfast (part of my pre-presentation routine-see Chapter 7). I asked a group of people who were sitting at a big, round table in the dining room if I could sit with them. They welcomed me, and then they resumed their conversation while I ate quietly and listened.

After a few minutes they started talking about the conference. Someone said, "What's the agenda for this morning?"

"So and so is starting at nine, and then they've got a motivational speaker at ten," the man to his right answered.

"Not another one of those guys," someone else groaned. "They think they know everything, but they're such losers, and then they come in here and think they can motivate us." Everyone was laughing, and I laughed along with them.

Then one man said, "Look, I've got it handled. You know my wife's pregnant, and she's not due for another month, but don't tell anybody. This guy starts at ten? I'll just tell my wife to page me with '911' at 10:05."

Everyone laughed even harder at that, including me. Finally, someone in the group asked me, "So, what do you with the company?"

"I'm not with the company," I said.

"Oh, so what are you doing here?" he asked.

"I'm the motivational speaker!" I replied, chuckling. Needless to say, the table got very quiet at that point, until I joked around with them and made everyone comfortable again. (I also used this story to start my presentation that day!)

When you walk into a room to begin a presentation, can you assume that most people are eagerly waiting to hear your message? If you assume that, I have a bridge in Brooklyn that I'd like to sell you. As a speaker you should assume the opposite—that unless your audience has paid to hear you, they have very little interest in you or your message. Think about most of the meetings and/or presentations you've been to. How many of them were you looking forward to with anything other than dread (or at best as a break from an otherwise busy day)? And if you've done presentations yourself, how many times have you looked around the table and seen people on their laptops reading their e-mail, or doodling on paper, or having side conversations that have nothing to do with what you're saying, or just not paying attention to you at all?

Unless you're famous or people have paid to hear you speak, you need to spend the first few moments in front of the audience focusing their attention on you. Now, we said earlier that your focus of your presentation isn't you but the message you wish to convey, and ultimately that's true. But as a powerful presenter, the first thing you must do is draw your audience's attention. If you don't gain their attention right from the start, it will be very difficult to get it later. That's why the first step in the FIRE-UP System is to *Focus your audience's attention on you and your message.*

In Braveheart, when William Wallace galloped onto the battlefield he didn't start by yelling "Fight, brave Scots!" at the top of his lungs. Instead, he drew the attention of the troops by telling them who he was, then making a joke when some of the Scots didn't believe him. Wallace made sure he had everyone's attention before he began delivering his real message—that they should fight the English no matter what the odds. A powerful presenter must grab the attention of the audience first; otherwise, they'll never listen to anything else you have to say.

How do you grab the audience's attention? You start by doing the preparation described in the first part of this book: (1) creating your outcome; (2) preparing yourself mentally, emotionally, and physically; and (3) making sure your content is in alignment with the values of honesty and focusing on the audience's good. With that as your background, you're ready to utilize the four secrets of drawing and keeping your audience's attention.

Secret #1: Get yourself into the right emotional and physical state.

Remember the old adage about the importance of first impressions? As a speaker, it's absolutely accurate. Your audience will be judging you from the minute you appear. And a large part of that impression will be formed not by the way you dress, but by your emotional state. Do you look relaxed or nervous? Are you confident or afraid? Audiences are attracted to relaxed, confident speakers. Make sure you are feeling these emotions, and the audience will be drawn to you automatically.

As a speaker you need to make sure you're in your Optimal Performance Identity (OPI) and your OPI emotions before you open your mouth. (Take a look at Chapters 6 and 7 if you have any questions about getting yourself into your OPI emotions.) Most successful presenters have some sort of ritual that helps them access those emotions easily. Create your own ritual, and then use it right before you enter the room.

Secret #2: Take control in a friendly way.

Early on, your audience will be deciding if they should give you their attention or not. So you must take control of the group immediately: bring the focus of your audience toward you in a friendly and inviting manner. If you don't, the rest of your presentation will feel like you're walking uphill carrying a hundred-pound backpack. You need to enter the room knowing that you're in control, that the people are there to hear your message, and that you have something worthwhile to tell them.

When I say, "take charge," I don't mean to be egotistical, rude, or demanding. Ineffective speakers often resort to tricks like rapping on the podium or table, raising their voices over the entire crowd, repeating themselves endlessly ("Settle down, now-settle down!") commanding ("Focus, people!") or even insulting the audience. None of these strategies will work in the long term, and often they will cause your audience to tune out. I believe it's far more effective to be friendly yet firm.

As long as your emotional state is strong enough and you are centered in your state and your purpose, simply by walking in and standing in front of the group you can focus everyone's attention on you. But there are a few additional, simple strategies that can tell your audience that it's time to pay attention to you as a speaker.

- **Do a five-minute time check.** Many times you will be doing a presentation as part of a meeting in the middle of a business day. In these circumstances it can be difficult to gather the energy of a room. Your audience may be straggling in, and those who are there can be talking amongst themselves, making phone calls, checking e-mail on their laptops, leaving the room for coffee or to go to the restroom. Making a pre-presentation announcement of your start time is especially effective in these circumstances. Five minutes before you plan to start announce to the group in a warm, friendly voice, "We'll be starting in five minutes. Please begin to finish up any phone calls or e-mails you may be working on. Also, if you'd like to get some coffee or visit the restroom, please do it now. We want to make sure that we start on time so you can get the most from this presentation." Make another announcement one or two minutes before you are planning to start, asking people to close up their computers and turn off their cell phones. Your audience will appreciate this because they will be prepared for the start of your presentation. And you'll appreciate the fact that you don't have to compete with e-mail and coffee breaks!

- **Have someone introduce you.** As we discussed in Chapter 7, having someone introduce you is one of the easiest ways to gain an audience's attention. The best person is usually the group's leader (the manager, point person, senior salesperson, etc.). The leader can get the audience's attention, let them know why they're here, what the outcomes are for the presentation, what their expectations are of the audience in terms of participation, and a little bit about the speaker (that's you). If the leader is unavailable or unwilling to introduce you, you may ask another person from your team to get the audience's attention and introduce you. A good introduction can focus the audience and create a sense of importance about your presentation.

- **Take a few seconds to look over your audience.** A confident speaker who commands attention will walk to where he or she will be speaking and take a few seconds to look over the audience in a friendly way before beginning to speak.

*   **Start with a warm and sincere greeting.** Don't say, "It's a privilege to be here with you today," unless you really feel that way. If you start by saying something that the audience feels is insincere, you will lose their attention immediately. Even worse, they will question the other things you say during the rest of your presentation. Make sure that whatever greeting you use, you are connected to your words and really mean and feel what you are saying. And a smile is almost always welcome!

Secret #3: Create rapport early and maintain it throughout.

Your job as a persuasive presenter is to create a relationship with your audience, one where they are willing to listen to you and believe what you say. That relationship is your responsibility. You must create a connection with the customer, not the other way around. I don't have a lot of patience with presenters who complain about tough crowds or an apathetic audience. Usually the problem isn't with the crowd but with the presenter. The presenter hasn't done his/her homework, or isn't being flexible enough, or perhaps he or she is just having a bad day and just can't feel connected with the audience. Certainly, some audiences are more difficult than others, but if you've done your homework, if you understand your audience's wants, needs, and wounds, and you're willing to be flexible and sincere in your communication, then you should be able to connect even with a hostile or apathetic crowd.

The best way to connect is by sincerely caring about your audience and their needs. We've talked a great deal about this, but it should always be uppermost in your mind when you're in front of a group. Even if your audience is unresponsive or hostile, find something you can care about—like the belief that these people *really need* what you're bringing to them!

Another way to connect with your audience is to consciously work to develop rapport. Rapport is a sense of connection between people, and it's built by a combination of three things: *(1) shared interests*, (2) the *words* we use in common, and (3) the way we use our bodies—our *physiology*. We create rapport when we mirror and match our customers' key words, voice qualities, and body language. As a speaker, you can use these elements to create a sense of rapport and connection with each member of your audience, thereby making it much easier to gain and keep your audience's attention.

Shared interests. This is the way most of us create rapport: we ask questions and discover what we have in common with someone—this person is a parent and so are we, or we're both in the business of selling, or we went to college in California, and so on. Any kind of shared interest gives us something that we can talk about and develop a relationship around.

In presentations, you can create relationship by aligning yourself with the interests and goals of the group. If you know this group is focused on increasing its sales, you can mention that right up front. If the audience is dealing with a reorganization that's producing a lot of uncertainty, you can talk about how difficult such times can be, and acknowledge them for their efforts to date. Discovering and utilizing the interests of your audience should be a vital part of your preparation, and you can use these interests early in your presentation to help create that sense of rapport and connection.

Remember, however, that your interest must be sincere. Any sense that you are using your knowledge of their circumstances simply for your own benefit will turn an audience off immediately. Find something in common with them, acknowledge it sincerely, and use it to create a sense of connection and caring.

Words. As part of your research, look for any words, phrases, or slogans that the audience or the company uses consistently, so that you can refer to those words in your presentation. When I was doing a series of trainings for Cisco, for instance, the phrase that was used repeatedly was "customer success." I asked about this phrase and discovered that it was one of the company's core values, one that was driven home to every person in the company. So in my presentations I referred to "customer success" and other key Cisco words or phrases whenever I felt it was appropriate. It made me feel more like a member of the Cisco team, and made it far easier for me to connect with my audience.

But there's another way in which we can use words to connect at a subconscious way with our audience. As you learned in Chapter 6, human beings take in information in five "modalities" that correspond to the five senses. The three primary modalities are *visual* (seeing), *auditory* (hearing), and *kinesthetic* (feeling, both by touch and emotionally). Each of these modalities has different key words, voice qualities, and body language.

Here's a chart to help you see the differences between the three modalities.

While each of us makes use of all three modalities, there's usually one modality where we're most comfortable "hanging out," so to speak. Don't you know people who are quick, lively, animated, and who use words like "see," "bright," and "clear" a lot? And other people who are more deliberate and perhaps have a great speaking voice that's easy to listen to? And still others who seem be very in touch with their feelings, who move more slowly and seem to be most comfortable sitting down and relaxing? Take a look around you at your next meeting or family gathering, and see if you can tell which modality—visual, auditory, or kinesthetic—where different individuals in the group are most comfortable.

As presenters, we can develop connection with an audience by speaking to all *three* modalities during the course of our presentation. First, we need to tailor our content to communicate visually (paint a picture for them of the outcome), auditorially (tell them how it will benefit them and make sure they hear what you have to say), and kinesthetically (describe how great the outcome will make them feel). Second, we can use visual (see, clear, focus, bright, etc.), auditory (hear, tell, sound, rings true, etc.), and kinesthetic (sense, touch, feel, hot/cold, heavy/light, etc.) words in our presentation. Third, we can use our physiology to connect with the audience in all three modalities.

Physiology. Physiology, or body language, is one of the most effective and yet subtle ways of developing and maintaining rapport throughout your presentation. Luckily, everyone uses body language unconsciously to develop rapport. Have you ever been deep in conversation with someone and all of a sudden you noticed that you both were sitting in the exact same position? Maybe you were even using some of the same gestures and talking at the same rate of speed. All these things are indications that you both were in *physiological rapport* with each other. Most of us never notice this happening, but it's one of the strongest ways in which we develop a feeling of connection with another person.

You can create the same kind of physiological rapport with members of your audience by adopting elements of the three modalities—visual, auditory, and kinesthetic—and using them at various points in your presentation. Pick places where you can be animated, talk quickly, and use visually descriptive words-hallmarks of the visual modality—and notice which members of your audience seem to respond. At other times, speak more slowly, use pleasing tones, describe how things will *sound*, how people will be able to *tell* the difference after they achieve the outcome you're presenting, how this will *resonate* in other parts of the company. Look around and see if you can tell which people are most comfortable when you are speaking in the auditory modality. Then find places where you can pause, take a moment, and touch on the emotions that will arise when they make this change, how the new outcome will *feel* to them, and check out the members of your audience who respond to the kinesthetic modality. As you change modalities, your body language will shift automatically into the speed, pace, and actions of someone who is visual, auditory, or kinesthetic. And the members of your audience who "hang out" in each of those modalities will feel themselves connected to you—that is, in rapport.

Secret #4: Entertain and engage your audience.

As a presenter, your task is to move your audience to take action on a predetermined outcome. But the *art* of presenting comes from how you move the group from where they are to where you want them to be. And the most effective way to move your audience is to entertain them and engage their emotions. Keeping your audience entertained and engaged will hold their focus and help them hear what you have to say.

I don't mean you have to turn into a stand-up comedian—very few of us have that level of skill and mental dexterity. But there are many ways to keep your audience entertained and engaged. *Variety* is one of the best. The worst thing you can do as a presenter is start off in one tone or one speed and never vary your delivery—that's a recipe for boredom. You want to use all the tools at your disposal to provide your audience with variety. Use slides, graphics, or other visual elements. Move around the room. Tell a story that makes a point or touches the emotions.

Shifting modalities constantly between visual, auditory, and kinesthetic is essential for keeping your audience entertained and engaged. Staying in one modality for any length of time will turn off a large part of your audience because you're not "speaking" their language. Even if you're in the visual modality, which is lively, with lots of energy and gestures, if you stay in visual for more than a few minutes you will trance people out. You need to go easily from visual to auditory to kinesthetic, and enjoy using all three modes. Then you not only create rapport with different parts of your audience, but you will also add spice to what you are saying and keep your audience on their collective toes.

Here are four other ways to engage your audience and involve them in your presentation.

1. **Request responses and feedback from your audience.**
   I suggest that you use a greeting or ask a question that elicits a response from the audience early on. For instance, when you first get in front of the group, say, "Good morning" or "Good afternoon," and see what kind of response you get. If your audience doesn't respond or if they respond poorly, do not proceed further. If all you get is blank stares and silence and you plunge ahead anyway, you're telling your audience that it's okay for them not to respond to you. In those circumstances, I use a little humor and say something like, "Hey guys, I know you're there. Let's try again." I say it in a light, playful way, but I make it clear that I'm asking them to respond. By the second time the audience will usually play along-as long as your attitude is one of playfulness rather than put-down.

2. **Ask questions during your presentation.**

    These can be questions designed to (1) create discussion ("What kind of improvement do you feel needs to be made for this team to reach its goals?"), (2) elicit individual or group responses ("What part could you play in that goal?"), (3) create general agreement ("Once you've decided on a goal, the next step is to make a plan, right?"), and/or (4) ensure everyone is on the same page ("Does that make sense?" "Is everyone clear?"). Anytime you ask a question, it helps keep your audience engaged— as long as you genuinely want, and require, an answer. A lot of presenters are great at asking questions, but they don't wait for an answer. Worse yet, it's very clear that they really aren't interested in the responses, and not paying attention to your audience is one of the fastest ways to alienate them. If you ask questions you truly want answers to, and incorporate those answers into your content, then your presentation will become a dialogue rather than a monologue, and your audience will be an equal partner in your joint success.

3. **Tell your audience how to get the most from your presentation.**

    Telling your audience up front how they can get the most from your session is a great way to create a "win" for both of you. Remember, your audience is giving you something very precious—their time—and they want to maximize the benefits of the session. As a speaker you can use this to your advantage. I often say something like, "I know your time is valuable, and I'm committed one hundred percent to making the best use of our session together. I'll tell you exactly how you can get the most of the next hour. But for this to work, I need your commitment to focus on what I'll be sharing with you, and to participate fully in what we'll be doing together. If you do that, then I promise you will leave here with tons and tons of value. Will you commit to giving your full focus and attention for the next hour?"

4. **Talk to individuals, not just to the group.**
   As I said in Chapter 1, a presentation is simply a series of connected conversations. When you first start speaking, it's fine to do a "scan" of everyone, looking over the group as a whole. But after that, it's far more effective to think of your presentation as a chance to talk for a few moments with each individual in the group. Direct a few sentences to one person, then move to someone else. When you have the attitude of speaking conversationally with each person in your audience, you create a far more intimate and effective communication. You're speaking with people rather than talking at them.

In truth, everything we've discussed in this chapter is very easy to accomplish, and actually occurs in the first two to three minutes of your presentation. Your goal is to establish a relationship with your audience, to create a connection and a sense that you're someone they are willing to listen to. As I'm sure your mother told you when you were growing up, first impressions are important; and the first step of the FIRE-UP System—*Focusing your audience's attention on you*—is designed to create a great first impression so you can move easily to the next step up the ladder of your presentation.

Chapter 10 Highlights

As a powerful presenter, you must focus your audience's attention on you and your message. The four secrets of doing this are:

- **Secret #1:** Get yourself into the right emotional and physical state. Access your OPI and OPI emotions before you get in front of your audience.

- **Secret #2:** Take control in a friendly yet firm way by (1) announcing a five-minute time check, (2) having someone introduce you, (3) taking a few seconds to look over your audience before you speak, and (4) starting with a warm and sincere greeting.

- **Secret #3:** Create rapport early and maintain it throughout. The best way to connect is by sincerely caring about your audience and their needs. Connection also is built by (1) shared interests, (2) words, and (3) physiology. Use the hints in this chapter to develop rapport consciously with your audience.

- **Secret #4:** Entertain and engage your audience. Use variety, stories, shifting modalities between visual, auditory, and kinesthetic, etc. Other ways to create variety include (1) requesting responses and feedback from your audience; (2) asking questions of your audience, (3) telling your audience how to get the most from your presentation, and (4) talking to individuals, not just to the group.

Chapter Eleven
I = Inform Your Audience of Your Purpose

Focus on Your Outcome!

Propose a commitment and close with emotion ←

Use their uniqueness to demonstrate a solution ←

Educate, empower and entertain your audience ←

Remind your audience of their pain ←

Inform your audience of your purpose ←

Focus your audience's attention on you ←

I N T E G R I T Y — I N T E G R I T Y

Preparation

My wife and I once went to hear a very well known speaker and author in the personal development field. I love this author's books, and I was very excited to hear him speak. But when this gentleman came onstage he said, "I don't have any agenda today. I'm just going to get up here and talk on whatever comes to my mind and just let it flow." And he did–he'd talk about one thing and then go on to a different topic that seemed completely unrelated to what he was saying earlier. I kept trying to take notes and follow the thread of what he was saying, but it was almost impossible. The speaker was funny and entertaining, but my mind was wandering all over the place. Nothing he said allowed me to connect what he was talking about to an outcome or reason why we were there. At the end of his talk, I turned to my wife and asked, "Did you enjoy that?" "No," she said. I hadn't either–we were both frustrated and confused. We had to work way too hard to follow the speaker, and we both just tuned out.

As we said in the last chapter, your first task is to get the audience's attention. But once you have it, you need to give them a reason to *keep* focused on you. You want to make it enjoyable, easy, and compelling for them to listen to what you have to say, by giving them reasons right up front for staying with you both physically and mentally. Your next step is to *Inform your audience of your purpose.*

Here are four reasons you must inform your audience of your purpose as soon as you have their attention.

1. Every audience is wondering what the presentation is going to be about and, more important, what's in it for them. You need to let them know up front what they can expect from you, and the value you will add to their day, their lives, or their company. By informing your audience of your purpose immediately, you are telling them, "I value your time and I promise to use it wisely." You also are setting up very clear expectations for what your presentation is about and how it will be of benefit to them. Everything in your presentation needs to be focused on benefits for your audience, and that starts by informing them of your purpose for being in front of them today.

2. Some people in your audience may have pre-existing concerns about you, the organization or firm you represent, or the solution you will be offering to their problem. If you allay those concerns immediately, you eliminate much of the resistance to what you have to offer.

3. Other people in the audience may not even want to be there. By letting your audience know your purpose for the talk and how you plan to add value, you can give even reluctant attendees a reason to pay attention to you for the duration of your presentation.

4. By informing your audience of your purpose first, you help ensure that they will be interested in what you have to say before you get into the rest of your presentation.

One of the best ways I've found for informing your audience of your purpose is with a *positioning statement.* In marketing, a positioning statement is a way of telling your customers who you are, what you do, and what value you will provide. A good positioning statement is a way of "owning" a particular piece of the customer's mind. It can help you win over your audience immediately, so they will be open to what you have to say. Using a positioning statement means less effort for you, more cooperation from your audience and a better result for your presentation.

Here's an example of a positioning statement a representative of XYZ Technology used in a presentation to the Information Systems department of a large corporation.

> *At XYZ Technology we see our role as a partner who is always looking for ways to improve your business. My goal today is to share some ways that we can solve the problems you have been experiencing with network reliability. In addition, I will be making you aware of three ways you can reduce your costs and significantly improve your productivity and profitability with a new XYZ network. I'd like to start by addressing some of the challenges you are facing with your current technology.*

If you were a member of this department, would this positioning statement give you a reason to pay attention? You bet. The speaker has told you he's there to solve your problems with network reliability. He's going to show you how to reduce costs and improve productivity and profitability. And he's going to talk about what he sees as the network challenges you're going through at the moment. The speaker has positioned himself as the answer to your specific problems-a great reason for you to keep listening.

Creating your own positioning statement is like devising the OPI (optimal performance identity) you developed in Chapter 6.

There are seven keys to a powerful positioning statement.

1. **It must be BRIEF.** The positioning statement should last no more than a minute or two in your presentation.

2. **It must be CLEAR ABOUT OUTCOME.** Let them know why you are there and what you hope to accomplish. (Since you created a clear outcome for your presentation in Chapter 4, this should be easy.)

3. **It must be HONEST.** Nothing turns an audience off faster that if they feel they're being lied to or manipulated. You can't say you're going to do one thing but have an ulterior motive-promising something for "free" and then trying to sell something on the back end, for example. You must be clear and honest about your outcome for the presentation, whether it is to sell something, teach something, or to get your audience to take a specific action.

4. **It must be NON-THREATENING.** Have you ever heard a speaker say something like, "Today I want to make sure you make the decision to choose my company for this project, and I'm not leaving until I hear yes"? Most people would put up walls and stop listening immediately. Your positioning statement should enroll, not threaten. What if the same speaker said, "Today I want to share with you some things that I think could improve your company and show you how we can help you do so"?

The outcome is the same in both statements, but in the second statement the speaker is inviting, not forcing, the audience to make a decision.

5. **It must CREATE INTEREST.** Your positioning statement must make your audience want to listen to you, by speaking to their needs and desires. You can use the information you gathered in creating your outcome to make sure your positioning statement is specific to this audience and its unique situation.

6. **It must PRE-FRAME any potential challenges or objections.** "Pre-framing" describes the process of answering potential questions, challenges, or objections before the audience can bring them up. All good salespeople know how important it is to handle objections in advance, and you can use your positioning statement to get rid of any reasons the audience may have for not paying attention to your presentation.

Examples of possible issues you can handle through pre-framing include:

- *Technical people who may try to challenge you to show that they know more than you.*
- *Someone who feels threatened by your solution.*
- *An audience that may be very price conscious.*
- *An audience that may be experiencing problems or dissatisfaction with a product that you have sold them in the past.*

In each of these cases, it's best to handle the objections immediately, so you and your audience can proceed with a clear field. You pre-frame by doing three things. First, *state the problem/ objection right up front*. If you have people in your audience that you know are technical experts who love to show off how much they know (and how little you know in comparison), you could say something like, "I know that there are some people in the audience who are experts in network security." If there's someone who may feel threatened by your solution, say, "I imagine there are people in this room who are uncertain about the impact of the solution we are suggesting" (a non-threatening way of putting it).

Second, *acknowledge the individual(s) for what they bring to the table*. Objections are a valuable part of the process of communication, and if one member of the audience has an objection or concern, you can bet that other members of the audience have it, too. So anyone who raises a concern can be your ally in the persuasion process. In the case of the technical expert, you might say, "You know as much or more about network security as I do, and it is an honor to have you in the room today." For a price conscious audience, you could say, "In these days, fiscal responsibility and attention to the bottom line are absolutely essential, and you're to be commended for making sure you get the greatest value for your money." This statement will help them feel better about investing in the (valuable) option you will be offering them.

Third, *refocus them on your outcome for the day and offer the objectors an alternative way of being heard*. In the case of the technical expert, you could say something like, "My goal today is to share with you specifically how our new security program can make your network virtually impenetrable. If there are questions that you have that will help the whole group understand our solution better, please ask them during the presentation. If, on the other hand, you have questions or comments that don't necessarily benefit the whole group, I will stay around afterwards to talk with you individually. This way we can make the most of the time we have here."

If your audience has had a problem with your company in the past, you *must* handle their objections immediately and definitely, by letting them know what's being done to fix the problem. In such a case, I might say, "We know that you have been experiencing challenges with the operating system created by our company. We've identified four issues that we believe have been causing the problems, and here's how we're moving forward on each of those issues. *(Then I explain what's being done to correct the problem.)* I just want you to know we're making progress on your challenges, so now we can focus on this."

7. **Finally, your positioning statement must position you to take the NEXT STEP.** It must lead very naturally into the next rung of our ladder, to Remind your audience of their pain.

Now it's time for you to write your own positioning statement. You might find it useful to review your notes from Chapter 4 to make sure you are clear about your outcome and the audience's wants, needs, and desires.

Exercise

Think about an upcoming presentation you will be making and write your own positioning statement. Make sure it uses each of the seven criteria for a great position statement as outlined in this chapter. If you know you have objections that must be handled, make sure to include pre-frames in your statement that will handle any challenges that may arise.

_____

_____

_____

_____

_____

A clear, dynamic positioning statement makes maximum use of the attention your audience is giving you, because you are telling them clearly why you are there and why they should continue to listen to you. It allows you to state your outcome clearly, concisely, quickly, and powerfully. And it makes it even easier to take the next step up the FIRE-UP ladder.

Chapter 11 Highlights

• You must give your audience reasons for staying with you both physically and mentally by informing them of your purpose. Use a positioning statement, telling them who you are, what you do, and what value you will provide.

• A good positioning statement must:
 1. be brief
 2. be clear about the outcome
 3. be honest
 4. be non-threatening
 5. make the audience want to listen to you
 6. answer any potential challenges or objections in advance by doing the following:
    • state the problem/objection right up front
    • acknowledge the individual(s) for what they bring to the table
    • refocus them on your outcome for the day, and offer the objectors an alternative way of being heard
 7. position your audience to take the next step.

Chapter Twelve
R = Remind Your Audience of Their Pain

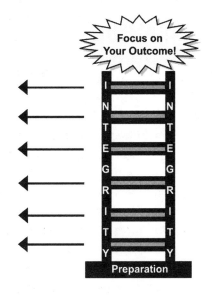

Propose a commitment and close with emotion

Use their uniqueness to demonstrate a solution

Educate, empower and entertain your audience

Remind your audience of their pain

Inform your audience of your purpose

Focus your audience's attention on you

Focus on Your Outcome!

INTEGRITY

Preparation

One hot, summer day a salesman was traveling along the back roads of the South. Feeling thirsty, he stopped at an old, dilapidated country store to get a soda. As he walked up onto the porch of the store, he noticed a hound dog lying at the end of the porch. The dog was whimpering and howling as if it was in pain. The salesman went in the store and asked for a soda. As the storekeeper brought it to him, the salesman said, "That your dog out there?"

"Yep," the storekeeper said. "He's always on the porch."

"Well, I think something's wrong with him," the salesman said. "He sounds like he's hurting."

"Don't think so," the storekeeper replied. "I checked on him a few minutes ago."

"But he's howling," the salesman protested.

"That's just 'cuz he's sitting on a nail," the storekeeper said.

The salesman looked at the storekeeper, surprised. "If the dog's sitting on a nail and it's hurting him, why doesn't he get up and move?"

The storekeeper shrugged. "It doesn't hurt him that bad!" he said.

As persuasive presenters, our job is to move people to take action. But people need a very strong reason to make any kind of change, and for most of us pain is a more effective motivator than pleasure. *People and organizations are motivated most by the desire to avoid pain.* To be an effective presenter you must take the next step in the FIRE-UP ladder: To *Remind your audience of their pain.*

This step can be difficult for many presenters, because most of us don't like to cause others pain. We feel it's negative; it brings up issues we don't want to deal with; it may cause our audiences not to "like" us for the moment. But if your audience is not experiencing pain, they will have little motivation to buy your solution to their problems. You can talk about how great your product is and how much value it provides, and your audience can still say, "Yeah, it's great, but we don't need it. Our company is doing fine." But if you remind them up front about how they've been losing money because of their antiquated communications or computers or customer service training strategies, and how their customers are choosing other companies due to their problems, then your audience is far more likely to listen to the solutions you're providing and to see your product or service as something they need rather than something they just would like to have. *Reminding audiences of their pain is the only way to move them from desiring your product or service to needing your product or service.* Remember, no pain, no gain! Or as salespeople say, "No pain, no purchase order."

Even if members of the audience have expressed their pain to you in the past, you can't assume it is in the forefront of their minds during your presentation. You must take responsibility for *reminding* them of their pain in the present moment. In your preparatory work you should have discovered your audience's problems, wants, and needs. Now is the time to use that information to remind your audience of what is not working in their lives or their business. Mention the fact that they're losing market share. Disclose that you've heard about the problems they're having with teamwork. Remind them of the big contract they lost because they couldn't deliver in a timely manner. By covering briefly the problems and wounds experienced by your audience, you bring their pain to the forefront of their minds, thereby helping them to be more receptive to your ideas and solutions.

When you remind your audience of their pain, you also position yourself and your product or service as someone who can help rid them of their pain. You become the "white knight" riding to their rescue. It's important, therefore, that every problem or pain you mention should be related to the solution you will be providing through your product or service.

In reminding the audience of their pain, however, you must have the right strategy. I've seen some presenters who tell their audiences how stupid it is that they have these problems, how much damage they've done by not addressing this problem sooner, and so on. They alienate the audience by making them feel hopeless. This is *not* the way to remind people of their pain! You want to make sure that you maintain rapport with your audience by using strategies that align with them rather than blaming them.

In my years as a presenter, I have found that the following four strategies are extremely effective in reminding audiences of their pain while maintaining a strong connection.

Strategy #1: Attack and confess.

With this strategy, you start by bringing up a problem that you or your company also used to have. This strategy allows you to demonstrate that you understand the challenges the audience is facing. You're also willing to be "up front" with them and tell it like it is. That's the attack part. But pointing out problems can alienate your audience unless you follow it by confessing that you (or your company) have had the same challenges. This causes your audience to accept your earlier attack as something designed to help them rather than as a put-down or accusation.

For example, when I train speakers, I'll often start by saying, "Many of you have been asked to do a presentation in front of a group of people, and you've had a bad experience. You either were so afraid that you refused to make the speech, and maybe you lost a promotion or a sale as a result. Or perhaps you made the speech and did such a lousy job that you thought you would never be a good speaker. I know that feeling. Early in my career, I had to get up in front of three thousand people and introduce one of the best motivational speakers in the country. And I was awful! I could barely be heard, I stumbled over my words, I forgot what I was going to say, and I almost tripped leaving the stage. I was absolutely the worst example of a public speaker that you could imagine. That's when I made the commitment to learn as much as I could about being a persuasive, dynamic speaker. And that's why we're here today: so you too can overcome your fears and learn to be confident, persuasive speakers in any situation."

Attack and confess is not about your pouring your own problems out to your audience. The reason for telling your story is to give your audience a reference so they start identifying the problem and seeing it as their own. You create a feeling of camaraderie and respect, as well as a sense in your audience that you understand their problems and can help them find a solution.

Strategy #2: Tell a third party story.

This strategy allows you to bring up a problem the organization has by telling a story about another organization with the same problem. A friend of mine is a consultant in the area of customer service, and not too long ago she was doing a presentation to the executives for one of the biggest telecommunications companies in the U.S. She had done her research and knew that call response time was the biggest complaint of the company's customers. So when it came time to remind her audience of their pain, she said,

"In the telecommunications industry, customer service is seen by most people as an oxymoron-a contradiction in terms. On a scale of one to ten, with one being the lowest, the industry as a whole receives an average rating of two on its customer service. Customers are spending an average of eleven minutes and 43 seconds on hold before someone answers their call. Once their call is answered, only 20 percent of their complaints can be handled by the first person they speak to. The other 80 percent are transferred to a second representative, who takes another six minutes 24 seconds before picking up. Industry wide, customers are spending an average of eighteen minutes waiting to speak to someone who can help them—and this from companies whose business is telecommunications!" In just about a minute, my friend had laid out exactly what the problem was with their customer service; she had reminded her audience of their pain by using a third party story which directly related to her audience.

She ended her third party story by saying, "In my prior conversations with your management team, they told me that these are the same issues you face. I'm here today to offer some solutions that will create world-class customer service in your company."

When you tell a third party story, you need to accentuate the problem so your audience understands the gravity and consequences of that situation. But don't embellish your story too much. Audiences have very sensitive "authenticity meters," and they will tend to doubt anything that seems like an exaggeration of the truth. You can underline or emphasize a problem, like my friend did by describing the effects of slow customer response. But don't make things worse or better than they actually are.

Strategy #3: Be direct but caring.

I call this the "tell it like it is" strategy: you address the company's problems directly, but without condemning them or putting them down. For example, "Your department has some issues with teambuilding that we've identified in working with you. We're here to fix them. The issues that we see that you can improve upon are communication between team members, clearer goals that are supported by every member of the team, and a game plan that allows for more accurate measurements of success." The key is to outline the problems without making your audience feel as if they have failed, while letting them know that you care and you're there to be of help.

Strategy #4: Ask questions.

This strategy allows you to get your audience to express their pain. If you can get your audience to tell you what's wrong, then they're already invested in finding a solution. As every salesperson knows, if you say it, the audience can doubt it; if the audience tells it to you, then it's the truth.

The key to successful questions is the old attorney's adage: *Never ask a question you don't already know the answer to.* A persuasive presenter uses questions to guide the audience to reach certain foregone conclusions about their pain, their needs, and the solutions the presenter is there to provide. If you've done your research and you know your audience, asking questions to lead them to recognize their pain is easy. You're asking questions you already know the answers to, but you're getting your audience to express their own pain in the present moment.

An example of a software salesperson using questions to sell a new network operating system may be as follows.

Salesperson: *"Paula, how often is your current network down or inoperable?"*
Customer: *"Three or four times a week."*
Salesperson: *"When the network goes down, approximately how long does it take to get it back up and working again?"*
Customer: *"It takes us about 45 minutes per occurrence on average."*
Salesperson: *"During those 45 minutes that it takes to get the network back up, what are the consequences that the business has to suffer?"*

Customer: *"Our team members can't access documents on our servers. Customer service can't function properly. And our online and offline sales processing system is shut down."*
Salesperson: *"Have you calculated what each occurrence costs you in real and opportunity costs?"*
Customer: *"We estimate that it costs us approximately $10,000 every time our network goes down."*
Salesperson: *"That's a lot of money that you don't have to be losing. The good news is we can help solve your problem and that's why I'm here today."*

Let me give you a personal example. I've worn contacts since I was 18 years old, but I never liked wearing them. And as I was developing my career as a presenter, I found that wearing contacts onstage was creating problems. The air conditioning in the rooms where I was speaking would dry my lenses out, and I couldn't leave in the middle of a presentation to put in more contact lens solution. I tried speaking without contacts, but my eyesight was so bad that I couldn't see my audience—and trying to have a series of connected conversations is pretty difficult when you can't see the people you're talking to!

About seven years ago I was in so much pain that I started looking around for solutions. I had heard about laser eye surgery but the idea of someone fooling around with my eyes didn't appeal to me. However, after a speech in Miami where the air conditioning was blowing directly on my eyes and I spent the entire speech with my eyes hurting because my contacts were so dry, I decided I had to get the surgery done—now. As soon as I got home to San Diego, I flipped open the Yellow Pages and called the doctor with the biggest ad for laser eye surgery. (I know, that's a really bad way to pick a doctor, but I didn't know of any eye doctors, and I was desperate.) I took the first available appointment, which was on Saturday.

When I arrived, the doctor's office looked like a "cattle call" audition for a movie. There were people everywhere—sitting in chairs, standing against the walls, lined up in the hallway. The receptionist called out four names at a time. When my name was called, I and three other people went into a small room off the hallway, where an assistant asked us to sit down and watch an informational video before the doctor met with us. The first part of the video was great—it showed all the benefits of the surgery, how it could give people 20/20 vision, how many people had had the procedure safely, and so on. Then came the down side: the potential side effects. They mentioned several, but I really only remember one, BLINDNESS! At this point all my fears about surgery on my eyes came rushing back. Do you think I was ready to go for the surgery? No way.

Then the doctor came into the room. At this point, I wasn't interested in the surgery, only in getting out of there as quickly as possible, but I felt I should be polite. The doctor (who looked completely worn out) shook my hand and said, "You look like a good candidate, do you have any questions?"

"Just one," I said. "Can you really go blind?"

"Well, it's possible," he replied. Not what I wanted to hear! But instead of allaying my fears, the doctor said, "The nurse will talk to you about schedules and financing," and he left the room. At this point, I was heading for the door, swearing I would never, ever get this done. The pain of the solution was much greater than the pain of my current condition.

That was true for a while—until the next time I went onstage and my eyes hurt the entire time because of my contacts. I thought, I don't care if I do go blind: I can't take this pain every time I give a speech. So when I got home, I made an appointment with a different doctor. Luckily, this doctor was much better versed in how to use pain and pleasure to persuade people to take action. At the doctor's office I was shown the same video about laser eye surgery (needless to say, it didn't put me in the best state). But when the doctor came in, he sat down with me and asked a series of questions. How long I had worn contacts. What kinds of activities I liked to do. What problems I was having with my contacts. Why I was considering laser surgery. I felt this doctor really wanted to understand my wants, needs, and desires.

After he did an eye exam, the doctor said, "Mr. McCarthy, you said you felt pain in your eyes when you were onstage for a speech. On a scale of one to ten, with ten being the highest, how badly do your eyes hurt when you're onstage?"

"Level eight," I said.

"And what part of the eye hurts?" he asked.

"The whole thing!" I replied.

"And what does that pain feel like?"

"It's like something's scratching my eye, or like I had glass in it." My eyes were starting to tear up just thinking about it.

"And this happens every time you're onstage?"

"Every time," I answered.

"And when's your next speaking engagement?" he asked.

"Next week," I said with a wince.

With just a few questions, this doctor had gotten me to associate fully to the pain of not taking action. He had done so respectfully, with integrity, and I felt as if he really cared about me and my welfare. I was completely ready to hear his possible solution.

"Well, Mr. McCarthy, taking a look at your chart I'm confident that this surgery can take care of your eyes," the doctor told me. "I also believe we can get you an appointment prior to your next talk. You told me that you have some hesitations about the surgery, so I'd recommend we do one eye the first time—the one with less vision problems—and restore it to 20/20 vision. Then we can take our time on the second eye and make sure that it's done absolutely right. How does that sound?"

I signed up that day and had the first surgery three days later. Today my eyes are both 20/20 and I'm delighted that I made the decision to have the surgery. I ended up paying more than I would have with the first doctor, but it didn't matter. I had made the decision to go ahead because the second doctor understood how to use pain to move me to action.

FIRE-UP Your Presentations & FIRE-UP Your Results

As a persuasive presenter, your ability to remind your audience of their pain and to get them to feel it in the moment will often make the difference between them saying, "Let's do it!" and "We'll think about it." If you want to move your audience to action, pain can be your best ally—as long as it's used with skill and caring.

Exercise

Using the chart below, write customer's potential pain as you know it from your preparation. Then identify a strategy you could use to focus the customer on that pain, and write how you would use that strategy in your presentation. If you want, use all four strategies so you can get practice in all of them.

If you've done your job in terms of building rapport with your audience, letting them know who you are and that you know who they are, and reminding them of their pain, you're ready to move into the core of your presentation: the content that will describe your solution to their problems. But your content must be more than dry facts. You must take the next

Problem	Strategy to Access Pain in Your Audience
Example: Inefficient delivery of HR benefits	**Strategy:** Attack & Confess: Tell how you had the same problem when working in HR and the company was changing health care providers.
Example:	**Strategy:**
Example:	**Strategy:**
Example:	**Strategy:**

step up the FIRE-UP ladder and keep your audience with you as you journey from point A to point B.

Chapter 12 Highlights

Use what you discovered about your audience's problems, wants, and needs to *remind your audience of their pain* while maintaining a strong connection. Use the following four strategies.

1. **Attack and confess.** Bring up the group's problem, then confess you or your company have had the same challenge.

2. **Tell a third party story** about another organization with the same problem. Make sure your account is accurate and factual; don't make things worse or better than they actually were.

3. **Be direct, but caring.** Address the company's problems directly, but without putting them down.

4. **Ask questions.** Rather than you telling them, get the audience to tell you about their pain. However, never ask a question you don't already know the answer to.

Chapter Thirteen
E = Educate, Empower, and Entertain
Your Audience

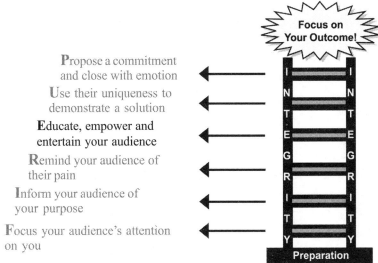

Propose a commitment and close with emotion

Use their uniqueness to demonstrate a solution

Educate, empower and entertain your audience

Remind your audience of their pain

Inform your audience of your purpose

Focus your audience's attention on you

Focus on Your Outcome!

Preparation

We've reached what would be considered the "content" or "body" portion of your presentation—the meat of what you have to say. Everything you've done up to this point—Focusing your audience's attention on you, Informing them of your purpose, and Reminding them of their pain—is accomplished in the first few minutes. However, if you don't take these first three steps, you'll find the fourth step much harder, like trying to climb a ladder by putting your foot on the fourth rung first.

Most speakers consider the body of their presentation as strictly informational: they tell the audience about their product or service, or present their position or proposal in a clear and logical way. But remember, we're talking about persuasive presentations-and persuasion is 10 percent logic and 90 percent emotion. That's why step four in the FIRE-UP System is represented by three "E's," which stand for *Educate, Empower, and Entertain.*

This is the body of your talk. Your introduction (the first three steps) is usually three to five minutes, and your conclusion (steps five through seven) is another five to ten minutes. If your presentation is thirty minutes, then, you have fifteen to twenty minutes to accomplish the step of educating, empowering, and entertaining your audience.

As a persuasive presenter, you must *educate* your audience about their situation and the issues they face, as well as how your solution can help them. You provide them with valuable information concerning the issues you raised in step three (where you reminded them of their pain). But you must do more than just educating your audience if you want them to take action. You also have to give them the feeling of being *empowered* by your ideas and the solution you propose. You've got to show them what's possible, how they can improve their lives and/or business, and help them see how easy it will be for them to accomplish their goals if they take the action you are suggesting. Finally, you've got to make the process *enjoyable*, so they'll keep listening to what you have to say. Even if you're talking about the dullest or most detailed technical specifications, your presentation must always be interesting! Boring content will have virtually no impact. The more interesting you can make your content, the more successful you will be.

There are three guidelines for making your presentation educational, empowering, and entertaining. First, *keep your presentation informative yet lean.* The most important aspect of this section of your presentation is to *keep focused on your outcome.* Everything you say must be directed towards the outcome you have created—the action you wish your audience to take. You must constantly and consistently focus your audience's attention on the solution you will be proposing to their problems.

Once I sat in on a meeting where a salesperson for a new computer operating system was speaking with a group of senior managers. The salesperson obviously knew his product and was very excited about what it could do. He had full-color charts of features and pages of specifications; he spent twenty minutes talking about servers and LANs and long-distance networking potential. Finally one of the managers interrupted him. "Joe, this is all very interesting, but what's this going to mean in terms of our bottom line?" Joe hemmed and hawed, but couldn't provide a clear answer. His audience was educated about a lot of things, but not about what they needed to know to make the decision to buy. And Joe didn't get the order.

No matter how "cool" you think the features of your product or service or proposal, if they aren't tied to your audience's wants, needs, and desires they will get in the way of your presentation. Never overeducate people. You may be tempted to add information that you believe provides extra value, but anything that distracts your audience from your outcome is a barrier. The question you should ask in determining your content is "What does my audience need to know to move closer to the outcome?" As you're refining your content, ask, "Do I need this content to move my audience to my outcome?" If it's not needed, get rid of it.

I suggest that speakers have a list of three to seven key points they plan to cover in the body of their talk. Studies of how people learn have shown that we can retain no more than three to seven "chunks" of information at one time. So make sure your content can be grouped in sections that will make it easy for your audience to remember what you have to say.

Second, *keep tying the information back to your audience in a way that they feel empowered by what you say.* When a friend of mine bought her first PDA, she was really excited because the salesman had convinced her it would make her life so much easier. But once she got the thing home, it sat in her desk drawer for six months. She tried to set it up, but the process was complicated and time-consuming. Eventually she took the PDA back because she didn't feel empowered to make the best use of this new piece of technology. As a persuasive presenter, you need to make sure that your audience isn't just educated about your outcome, but they also feel *empowered* to accept that outcome and put it into action in their lives.

You can do this in several ways. First, use examples and language that cause the audience to see themselves solving their problems. Suppose I was the salesperson who sold my friend the PDA. When she came in the store, I would show her several PDAs and tell her all about what these devices could do. (Every persuasive presenter knows the importance of explaining the benefits of a product or service to the customer.) I'd say, "If you had one of these, your life would be a lot better." With just that information, I might get the sale—but my friend still wouldn't know how to operate the PDA and therefore I would not have empowered her. But what if, with each benefit, I spent a little more time to make sure she understood what the PDA could accomplish for her and her specific needs? Perhaps I helped her set up the first page of her calendar. Maybe I would give her my business card and tell her to call me or come back and see me if she had any problems with setting up the PDA. Do you think my friend would feel empowered to use her PDA? You bet. Would she be more likely to use it and not return it? Absolutely.

As a persuasive presenter, your audience has to feel that they can own the solution you are providing, that it will work for them and they can use it effectively. Knowledge without the ability to use it is frustrating. You must empower your audience to accept your outcome and take the action you wish them to take. *You start by putting them on a pedestal and making them feel important.* With my friend, I might say, "You're probably an extremely busy person and very interested in increasing your productivity—that's why you're looking at purchasing a PDA." In a corporate presentation, you might acknowledge the company's efforts to turn their customer service department around, or how they've been struggling against enormous odds to get orders delivered despite an antiquated order system.

Next, *target your empowering solutions to their problems.* Let's say my friend wants to have contact phone numbers immediately accessible, to be able to keep and update her calendar consistently, and to check her e-mail anytime, anywhere. What do you think I (as a persuasive presenter) will say? "In five minutes you and I can set up a contact file and a date book, and program your e-mail access into this device. You'll see how easy this PDA is to use." I've let her know I can help her immediately with her pain, and that she will be empowered to continue using the device when she takes it home. I didn't show her features of the PDA that she didn't consider important (although I would probably show her the features briefly before she left). I targeted my education to suit her needs and empowered her to take the action of using the PDA once she bought it.

Third, *use your skills to make the presentation entertaining.* Have you ever been in a thirty-minute presentation that seemed to last an hour? You want to have the opposite effect: your thirty-minute talk should feel like fifteen. If you can keep your audience entertained, they're more likely to stay focused on what you have to say, and more likely to take the action you desire.

If you're not a professional comedian or if speaking doesn't come naturally to you, take heart—being "entertaining" doesn't mean you have to do a song and dance, or tell great jokes. What entertaining really means is, first, *maintaining rapport with your audience.* We talked about developing rapport in Chapter 9, by using shared interests, sincere caring, specific words and patterns of physiology. Continue using these strategies to ensure the ongoing relationship between you and your audience. Check your audience constantly to make sure that you're still in rapport.

The second key to being entertaining is to *keep your audience emotionally involved.* Remember, decisions are made based on 10 percent logic and 90 percent emotion, not the other way round. Your content should trigger your audience's emotions as well as their minds. Here are seven tips for keeping your audience engaged and your presentation entertaining.

1. Use games, exercises, and examples.

Examples, games, and exercises make what you are talking about more real. They also get your audience more involved by making them a part of your presentation. Suppose you were presenting a new instant messaging software program to a company. The meeting is held in a big conference room, with everyone sitting around a table. You walk in, hand the person to your right a note, and ask him to pass it all the way around the group until it gets to the person who is sitting to your left. You keep talking while the note goes from hand to hand, eventually arriving at its destination. "How long did that take?" you ask. Then you take the note back and ask the person on your right to hand the note directly to the person on your left. He does so, and then you say, "That's the difference between e-mail and instant messaging. With e-mail, your message has to go through who knows how many computers and servers to get to its recipient. With this IM program, you can be in instantaneous contact with your salespeople, vendors, branch locations, different departments, whatever, anywhere around the world." Using a physical example of your product gets your audience to understand the benefits more directly.

Role-play can also be a very effective tool in keeping your audience engaged. "John, let's assume you're the customer, and Jane, you're at the branch office in Sydney, Australia. John, you have a problem you want Jane to solve with your account. What's the problem? Jane, you need to get an answer for John immediately. What would you have to do in order to reach the main office in the U.S.?" Examples, games, and exercises help make your product, service, or outcome more real to your audience.

Games and exercises also get people out of their head and into their physiology. When I do speaker trainings, I ask students to write down all the negative things they associate to public speaking. Then I ask them to pass the list to their neighbor, take their neighbor's list and stand up and read it at the top of their lungs in a Mickey Mouse voice. Everyone does this at the same time, so no one feels singled out or intimidated. This game helps people see how ridiculous their beliefs around public speaking are. It also really loosens up the crowd! Changing people's physiologies through games and exercises is one of the best ways to keep your audience entertained and engaged.

2. Ask questions.

We are trained to respond when someone asks us a question. Questions like, "Does that make sense?" "Does everybody understand that last point?" "What does this mean to you?" "Is that clear?", helps you to evaluate how much your audience is taking in from your presentation. I also like to ask questions about the points I'm making; this is a subtle way of letting the audience know that you are expecting them to pay attention to you and absorb what you have said. "So, Jim, how would this IM system increase your department's productivity?" "Karen, you work in customer service, and I know that response time to customer requests has been a challenge for this company. You use phone and e-mail to link CSRs with managers, right? Suppose a CSR was dealing with a particularly irate customer, what if the CSR could IM the manager and get an immediate response?" Questions help you connect your presentation with your audience by having *them tell you*, rather than you telling them.

3. Make statements that create anticipation in your audience.

"And the winner is . . . " Have you ever watched an award show and been caught up in the emotion of waiting for the winner to be announced? Anticipation can be one of your best tools when it comes to creating an entertaining presentation. You can set up anticipation by telling your audience that you're about to say something great or important. "Please listen to this next point." "Everybody needs to hear this." "This next feature could save your company at least a million dollars in the first year." "What I'm about to share with you now is the one thing all successful executives must implement in order to build strong teams." (Of course, you then need to fulfill these big promises with quality content.) Statements that create anticipation and curiosity will keep your audience focused on you and your content.

4. Vary your delivery.

Have you ever heard the expression "Keep 'em guessing?" If anticipation gets your audience interested, variety will keep them that way. Variety can make even the most tedious technical content more interesting and involving. You want to use as many tools as you can to stimulate your audience's senses. Colorful slides and video presentations can help, but for the most part you must create variety with your primary tools of voice, physiology, and movement.

Remember the three modalities—visual, auditory, and kinesthetic—we discussed in Chapter 9? Each modality has a different set of characteristics:

- *Visual:* Fast pace, volume, movement
- *Auditory:* Moderate pace, volume, movement
- *Kinesthetic:* Slow pace, volume, movement

Using all three modalities in your presentation will help you connect with the different people in your audience, as well as providing the variety that will keep them interested and engaged. You can use different modalities to help you make your points. Paint a visual picture for your audience of how much better their lives will be when they take the action you're advocating. Have them hear what their customers will say, or what they will say to themselves once they achieve the outcome of your presentation. Talk about how they will feel once they've made the decision; connect them to their emotions. Vary the speed and pacing of your rate of speech (fast for visual, more moderate for auditory, slow for kinesthetic). Using all three modalities will create enormous variety in your delivery. (See Chapter 15 for more on this topic.)

5. Use stories to convey your message.

Jesus knew all about the power of using a story to make a point. Stories not only teach and inform, but they are entertaining as well. And often they can make the point far more memorable than any explanation or technical information could. Stories can be drawn from many sources—books like *Chicken Soup for the Soul*, business books, magazines like *Readers Digest* or *Fortune,* or the latest edition of your local newspaper. Personal stories are always great, but you can use stories that have been told to you by friends, family, business associates, and so on. I suggest that speakers create a database of stories they can use depending on the occasion and the audience.

When you use a story as part of your presentation, you don't need to memorize it; just make sure you have the key elements of the story straight and, most important, that you're clear on the point you wish to make by telling the story. I will review a story several times so I have its main elements in my mind, and then I'll write one sentence to remind me of the story content and the point I want to make. Again, make sure your stories contribute to your outcome and use scenarios and characters your audience can relate to.

6. Put your focus on your audience, not inside your head.

Have you ever seen a speaker whose focus seems to be somewhere in the back of his eyes? He's in front of the group, but somehow you feel he isn't with you. Or have you ever seen someone who is constantly searching for what to say next? These kinds of behaviors mean the speaker is in his head rather than with his audience. He's focusing on things like how he's doing and what he says next, rather than looking at the audience and wondering how *they're* doing. While it's perfectly okay (and perfectly normal) to go inside your head every now and then while you're giving a presentation, 99 percent of the time your focus should be on your audience. The best way to keep your audience interested in you is for you to be interested in them. If ever you find yourself asking questions like, "How am I doing?" look at your audience and ask, "How are they doing?"

7. Use what your audience gives you.

Every audience is going to be different, and every one is going to present you with new, unique opportunities for what's called utilization—using whatever comes up to increase the connection, impact, and entertainment value of your presentation.

For example, suppose you're in the middle of your description of the advantages of a new line of digital recorders you want this company to purchase for all its salespeople. You notice one of the people in the room has a micro recorder on the table. You pick up the recorder and say, "Joe, say you were recording this meeting so your secretary could transcribe it later. You also dictated a few letters and memos on the other side of this tape. You'd have to take the tape out of the recorder, give it to your secretary, and then she's spend probably about three hours transcribing the 90 minutes of tape time, right?" Then you pick up your own digital recorder and say, "I've been recording my presentation, too, and after this meeting I'll make some verbal notes for follow-up actions. When I get home, I simply plug the recorder into a dock by my computer. I hit one key, and the digital audio file is automatically downloaded onto my hard drive. If I want to have a hard copy of my notes, I open up a transcribing program—which comes with the recorder, by the way—select the digital audio file, and the file is transcribed automatically by my computer. I can have the transcribed file in about five minutes, and I can get the transcription done anytime of the day or night." I've used Joe's micro recorder to strengthen my presentation and make my point even more forcefully.

You can use questions and comments from the audience, information you have researched about the company, even unexpected events like fire alarms and cell phones ringing, to increase the impact of your presentation rather than interrupt it. (If a cell phone rings, for instance, you could say something like, "If that's your competitor, tell him he's about to lose 50 percent of market share when you put this new product or system in place.") Whenever something occurs during a presentation, I'm always asking, "How can I use this?" And the answers often make my presentation even stronger.

Remember, however, that your content must not only entertain but also must educate and empower. Everything you say, every story you tell, every example, exercise, or game you use must move your audience toward your outcome—and to the solution for their problem that you will be proposing next!

Exercise
1. Write down the outcome for your presentation. (You should have created your outcome in Chapter 4.)

2. In light of that particular outcome, write down the key points you need to make to educate your audience.

_____

_____

_____

_____

_____

3. Describe at least three ways you could empower your audience to make use of the solution you will be providing them.

_____

_____

_____

_____

_____

4. Finally, come up with three ways you can make your presentation entertaining and engaging. Look at the seven tips described in this chapter for some ideas.

_____

_____

_____

_____

_____

_____

Chapter 13 Highlights

1. Persuasion is 10 % logic and 90 % emotion, so the body of your talk must educate, empower, and entertain your audience.

2. Keep your presentation informative yet lean, and focused on your outcome. Ask yourself, "What does my audience need to know to move closer to the outcome?" Create a list of three to seven key points for the body of your talk.

3. Make sure that your audience feels empowered to accept your outcome and put it into action. Make your audience feel important while you target your empowering solutions to their problems.

4. Make your presentation entertaining by keeping your audience emotionally involved.

   - Use games, exercises, or examples.
   - Ask questions.
   - Make statements that create anticipation in your audience.
   - Vary your delivery.
   - Tell stories that teach your message.
   - Put your focus on your audience, not inside your head.
   - Use what your audience gives you.

Chapter Fourteen
U = Use Your Audience's Uniqueness to Demonstrate a Solution to Their Problems

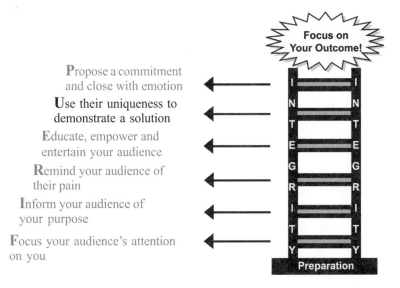

Propose a commitment
and close with emotion

Use their uniqueness to
demonstrate a solution

Educate, empower and
entertain your audience

Remind your audience of
their pain

Inform your audience of
your purpose

Focus your audience's attention
on you

Focus on
Your Outcome!

I N T E G R I T Y

Preparation

In the last step we talked about keeping your content focused on your outcome, and how everything must be linked in your audience's minds to their particular situation. Targeting your content specifically to your audience is also critical in the fifth step of the FIRE-UP System. You must use what you know about this audience, this company, this group, and their desires, needs, and most particularly, their pain, to demonstrate clearly and concisely how your outcome will help them. You must *Use your audience's uniqueness to demonstrate a solution to their problems.*

This step takes the audience's pain and shows specifically how your solution will get rid of it. You may use some of the content from the last step, but now you are focusing in on the *specific benefits* your solution will be providing. This is where your preparation and research come in: every time you present your solution, it must be tailored to the unique needs and pains of your audience. This step also readies the audience to be able to make a commitment (step six).

The hardest thing for most presenters to remember in this step is to be *specific* and target their solution to those aspects that will cure the audience's pain. The only parts of your solution that the audience truly cares about are the benefits that relieve the pain they feel.

Suppose John is speaking to a group of sales managers of XYZ company about a new customer order tracking system that can be used in the field to transmit orders directly to the home office. He goes on and on about how this program can be used on laptops, how it's absolutely cutting edge, how it can transmit orders instantaneously to a centralized computer system in the home office, where someone can process the orders immediately. He buries the audience with his descriptions of all the great benefits of using this system in the field. Finally, one of the sales managers interrupts. "John, that sounds great—but our salespeople are switching from laptops to PDAs and cell phones. In fact, we're looking to replace the programs we were using on the laptops because they won't work on the other equipment. Will this program work on those devices as well?"

"We have salespeople all over the world," another sales manager adds. "What happens if the orders come in at three in the morning? Does there have to be someone in the office to process the orders, or can the system automatically send the order to our plant?"

Oops! John knew that this company had challenges with order processing in the field and the home office, but he didn't know the company had switched over to PDAs. He also hadn't considered that the problems with order processing might have been caused by orders coming in around the clock. John was proposing a general solution for a company with unique problems. Unfortunately, his solution wasn't what the company needed, and he didn't get the sale.

As a presenter you can have a product with fifty different benefits, but the only thing your audience will care about is your answer to the question, "What do you have that's going to solve my problem?" Indeed, if your product or service has fifty different benefits and only ten of them apply to the audience, hearing about the other forty benefits may make them think, "I'm paying for a lot of stuff I don't need." And that's a thought you never want in your audience's mind.

There are four keys to creating and proposing a unique solution for your audience's pain.

1. **Customize your solution.** Make sure the solution you are proposing is tailored to the audience's wants, needs, and most important, the pain you uncovered in your preparation. Suppose you are selling a management training course that helps managers build great teams, and you know how important teamwork is to increasing productivity. But you also know that the biggest problem in this company is getting managers to report results in a timely manner. So you would create a version of your course that trains managers in taking responsibility, shows them how to create systems for reporting, and helps develop accountability throughout a department, allowing managers to get results from employees and deliver them to executives on time and with enthusiasm. The solution you are proposing is tailored to the unique needs and pain of your audience.

2. **Narrow in: focus on the benefits that apply to this audience, its unique needs and pain.** Even if your solution has some outstanding benefits that you love to talk about, don't mention them unless those benefits can be tied directly to the audience's pain. Assuming John had done his preparation and knew the needs of XYZ's sales force, he might have said to the managers, "With

this new order system you're going to get direct reporting from sales reps in the field to the home office, transmitted over any kind of device: PDA, cell phone, or laptop which will give you the versatility you need. The program at the home office will record all sales orders and send them immediately to distribution. Orders are reviewed when the sales order manager comes in, and any orders with problems are flagged and queries sent over the same system back to the sales reps in the field. But most orders are processed and sent directly to the plant around the clock enabling to significantly increase your productivity and effectiveness." The order system may be able to do all kinds of other things, but the only benefits John talks about are those that solve his audience's unique problems.

3. **Use tie-down questions as you present the solution to verify that your audience is with you.** As you learned in the last chapter, the human brain is wired to answer questions. Even when you are speaking to a very large audience and may not get individual responses to your questions, asking questions will cause them to respond inside their heads. Questions like, "Is that something you want?" "Can you see how this is going to work?" "Does everyone understand that?" "Does that make sense?" "Would that be helpful?" focus your audience's attention on how your solution will solve their problems. It will create ongoing agreement inside their heads, and also bring up any potential problems or issues that you might not have dealt with.

4. **Make sure your solution is win-win.** The solution you propose must work both for your audience and for you. If you're presenting a new $1 million computerized ordering system to a start-up company, and it will take three years to get the system online, that probably won't be a win for your audience. Conversely, if the solution

you're presenting doesn't cause you to get the sale, contract, or agreement—because they can get the same benefits somewhere else or do the same thing with their current resources—then the result won't be a win for you. Your solution must be a win for both sides as each side defines a "win." For you, it will probably be the audience accepting the outcome you created (which was win-win). For your audience, it will be a solution that solves their problem and gives them benefits targeted to their unique situation.

Exercise

1. Write down the pain your audience is experiencing and the benefit in your solution that will relieve the pain. I've included an example to illustrate how this works.

Pain: Current PBX system makes it very difficult and costly to move people from one office or station to another. **Solution Benefits:** Our telephone solution allows you to move from one office or station to another and transfer your extension, voice mail, and internet connection immediately with no additional cost.

_____

_____

_____

_____

_____

_____

_____

_____

2. Now, do the same thing for your audience's pain, providing
    solution benefits for every aspect. You may have more
    than one solution benefit for your audience's unique pain;
    however, make sure that you only include benefits that
    address the audience's pain—nothing else. Finally, check
    to determine if your solution and its benefits are a win for
    you and a win for your audience.

    If you present a solution based on the unique needs of your
audience, if your solution eliminates their pain, and if it is a win for
both you and the audience, then your next step will be the easiest of
all—getting them to commit to the action you wish them to take.

Pain:	Solution Benefit(s):	Win for both?
1.		_____ Yes _____ No
2.		_____ Yes _____ No
3.		_____ Yes _____ No
4.		_____ Yes _____ No
5.		_____ Yes _____ No

Chapter 14 Highlights

This step uses your audience's uniqueness to demonstrate a solution to their problems. You must be specific. Use these four keys.

1. Customize your solution.
2. Narrow in: talk only about the benefits of your solution that apply to this audience and its unique needs and pain.
3. Use tie-down questions as you present the solution to verify that your audience is with you.
4. Make sure your solution is win-win.

Chapter Fifteen
P = Propose a Commitment and Close With Connection

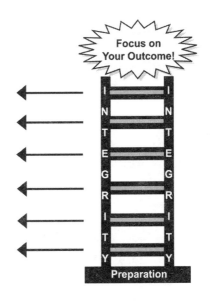

Propose a commitment
and close with emotion

Use their uniqueness to
demonstrate a solution

Educate, empower and
entertain your audience

Remind your audience of
their pain

Inform your audience of
your purpose

Focus your audience's attention
on you

Focus on
Your Outcome!

Preparation

You've now reached the culmination of your presentation. You've made your case and presented your solution which relieves your audience's pain; it's time to ask your audience to make a commitment to your outcome. But once you've gotten the commitment, your job isn't done. You need to connect your audience back to their emotions and make them feel great about the commitment they've made, and about you as the one who suggested the solution. Thus, the last step on the FIRE-UP ladder is *Propose a commitment and close with connection.*

If you've followed the first five steps of the FIRE-UP system, then the audience is probably already sold, and all you have to do is to solidify their commitment. But just like stepping on the rung at the top of a ladder, you still have to take care to ensure there are no last-minute slip-ups.

When you close your presentation, you must ask your audience to take some sort of action: to act on the point you're making, to purchase a particular product or service, to adopt an idea, to change a system or procedure to a new way of doing things, and so on.

When I train speakers, I always suggest that they enter this last step with the assumption that they have made their case effectively and the audience will take the proposed action. However, I also tell presenters to be prepared for any result that may arise.

There are four possible results presenters may encounter. Two of the results are black and white; the two others are ambivalent and require more effort on your part to bring them to a conclusion.

THE 4 RESULTS OF A PRESENTATION

POSITIVE	NEGATIVE
Commitment	No Agreement
Advance	Continuation

Positive Result #1: Commitment

This is the ideal result, when they say, "Let's do it right now and sign a contract." You've made your case effectively, you've proposed a solution based on their needs and their pain, and you've made it clear to them that the solution is in their best interests. Congratulations! All you need to do now is to thank them and affirm they have made the right choice.

Positive Result #2: Advance

Your audience sees the value in what you're presenting but they're not quite ready to make a commitment. You may hear things like, "We need to get with our VP to figure this aspect of the deal out, and then we should be ready to decide." Or, "This sounds great, but we need more information about the rollout schedule." Or, "We like your idea: can we run your numbers by our Chief Accounting Officer and get back to you?" It should be clear that your audience desires to make the commitment, but there is something standing in the way. (This is different from the "We'll get back to you" response, which we'll cover later.)

Your job as a presenter is to move your audience toward your outcome by asking them for a small commitment or series of smaller commitments. If they need more information, ask to set up another meeting to present it to them. If they say they must run your proposal past another committee or company member, ask to meet with those people by a certain day, if possible. The key to moving an advance to a commitment is *specificity*. Remember, as soon as you leave the room, your proposal becomes less urgent. Proposing a series of specific actions both you and the audience will take within set time frames helps keep your proposal in front of your audience's minds and moves them closer to commitment to your outcome.

Negative Result #1: No Agreement

"Thanks, but no thanks." For whatever reason, your audience isn't convinced of the solution you're proposing. Don't take this response personally: if you do enough presentations, you're going to get this response more than once. The only thing you can do is to try to discover the reasons the audience didn't accept your solution. The reasons could be practical (your solution costs too much and they're cutting back), due to timing (it's the end of their fiscal year and they have no more budget for training), or changes in their situation (a new vice president has just been appointed and she's put acquisitions on hold for six months).

All this is interesting, but what you are really looking to discover is if you could have done anything different or better to make the case for your outcome. I suggest that if you get a "no" response, you ask your contact person if you can call him or her in a day or so. On the phone, you ask your contact to be honest with you. Say you're not looking for anything other than feedback about your presentation, and how you could have done a better job in making your case. Be persistent but not pesky, and take everything you hear as if it were true, whether you feel it is or not. Even in the most biased and unfair feedback may be a grain of truth that you can learn from and become a better presenter as a result.

Negative Result #2: Continuation

"Let us think about it and we'll get back to you." This result often means "We don't want to tell you no to your face." Continuation is actually the worst result of the four. With a "no agreement" response, at least you know your result, and you can focus on your next presentation. With continuation, you think something is going to happen even though there's a 90 percent chance that it won't.

The way to deal with continuation is to move your audience from continuation to advance by getting a specific commitment. If you get the answer, "We'll think about it and get back to you," you can say something like, "I appreciate that—let's set a date when I can follow up with you. Is next Monday good?" If you get an ambiguous answer ("I don't know if we can have an answer by then"), you can respond with, "Great! Can you let me know when I can call you for an answer? Or is there something I can provide you with that will help you come to a decision?" Your goal is to maintain rapport while letting your audience know that you aren't willing to let them off the hook. Even a small commitment will help them move out of continuation and into one of the other three results.

When challenges or objections come up, often it's because you talked about the outcome way too early, and you haven't created enough pain in your audience's minds to move them to action. However, with the FIRE-UP System, you can revisit any of the steps during your close to reinforce their impact on your audience. If necessary, re-establish rapport and Focus their attention on you and your outcome (step one). Inform them again of your purpose in being there (step two). Remind them of the pain they currently have (step three-this is absolutely vital). Review the key points of your solution and how they are Empowered now to take action (step four). Recap the benefits of your solution and how it Uniquely handles their problems (step five). All of this can be accomplished in two minutes or less.

Five Steps to an Effective Close

As part of Proposing a commitment and closing with emotion, here are five steps to help you close the audience effectively:

Step 1. Check that you've addressed any key concerns.

This is your last, best opportunity to hear from your audience before you ask for the commitment. Some presenters are worried about allowing the audience to verbalize their concerns at the end of the presentation. "What if someone says something that blows the whole thing?" they ask. Well, if people have concerns, they will express them at some point, and no one is going to answer them like you will. Make sure your audience expresses their concerns while you're there so that you can handle the issues immediately.

You can elicit concerns by simply asking for them. "Are there any concerns you have that we haven't covered?" "Are there any questions you need to ask to help you make a decision about our solution?" Make sure you're looking at body language as well as listening to the audience's responses. Sometimes people are reluctant to be the first person to bring things up, but it's usually pretty easy to tell whether your audience is comfortable and confident with the solution you've provided. If they don't appear comfortable, probe a little: "I want to make sure this solution will work for you in every aspect. What do you need to know about to feel even better about our solution?" Then answer their concerns and emphasize how your solution will eliminate their pain.

Step 2. *Summarize the benefits of the proposed outcome.*

Go over the benefits again to remind them of what they will be getting by making the commitment. For example, "Our new network will lower expenses and increase your bottom line in the following ways . . ." Your summary can be short and sweet; however, make sure that everyone in the audience understands what you are reviewing.

Step 3. *Propose a realistic commitment or advance.*

This starts by asking for the audience's commitment to your outcome. If you get an enthusiastic "yes" or a firm "no," then you can move to step four. However, if you get either an advance or a continuation, you need to offer your audience a concrete next step. You can say something like, "I propose we set a meeting next week so I can answer the questions you've raised."

Make sure the commitment you propose is realistic in the audience's terms. If they have to run your solution by their senior management committee and the committee doesn't meet for another week, asking to get an answer before then probably isn't realistic. You also can ask your audience, "Keeping in mind the urgency of your situation, what do you see as the best next step?" If they give you feedback that is not what you are looking for, you can help mold it into what you want— "I propose that we have this new training plan in place within three weeks."

Sometimes you can ask the leader of the group to determine the next step. "Susan, what's the next thing we need to do to move this forward?" If the leader comes up with a commitment that is weak or inappropriate, you can suggest a better commitment and move them towards it. "Susan, I'm pleased that you would like to see another full proposal from me that takes into account training your sales staff nationally and internationally. I'll work on that; in the meantime, can I have your commitment to roll out a prototype program locally, so you can see the results of our training?"

The key to moving your audience from continuation to agreement is to ask for a series of commitments. When I speak to companies about my presentation trainings, I will ask, "How many of you are interested in this training? How many of you are committed to handling your fears about speaking and taking the next step now? How many of you are actually going to follow through? Even if something stops you, how many of you are going to do this?" I ask for commitment after commitment—a series of small yesses that move people ultimately to say yes to the solution I provide.

Step 4: Create a lasting connection.

It's an old axiom of sales that people buy from emotion and justify their decision with logic. So at the very end of your presentation, it's important to connect emotionally with your audience. Remember, a presentation is a transfer of emotion. You began your presentation by connecting with your audience even before you entered the room. You need to end your presentation in the same way, by connecting with your audience and showing them you care. Leave them with the feeling that you are committed to them beyond making a sale or gaining their commitment to an outcome.

One of the best ways to connect with your audience is by telling a story. This can be a story from your own life, or a story from the database you created to use in step four (Educate, empower, and entertain). Your story or anecdote should be something that relates to your audience or your outcome. For instance, if you're asking a group of managers to embrace a new way of doing things in your department, you could tell a story about your five-year-old going off to kindergarten for the first time. Or maybe a story about how you learned to snowboard after being a skier for years, and how you fell down constantly until your eight-year-old daughter taught you the secret of keeping your balance. Or a story about Franklin Roosevelt after he got polio, and how this brave man had to create a new way of influencing people that had nothing to do with physical might and everything to do with his mind and caring for people. The story you tell should be something you feel connected with, one you can tell with passion and that illustrates the outcome you wish your audience to adopt.

If you're not comfortable with telling a story or you don't have one that you feel is appropriate to the circumstances, don't worry. You can simply close with a few heartfelt, sincere words. Here's an example: "I appreciate your allowing me to speak with you today. We've been talking about a specific solution, but I want you to know I consider myself a supporter of your success. As we move forward I'm going to be looking at your business in any way that I can, to see how I can make it more successful. That's why I'm here." Sincerely caring for your audience and their success is a great way to close your presentation with connection.

Step 5: Finish at the peak!

I'm sure you've heard about the importance of first impressions; but when it comes to persuasive presentations, last impressions are equally important. How you end your presentation will be what the audience will take away with them. Ending with a thank you and a positive statement about your audience will leave them and you in a peak state. Remember, as the presenter you are in control of the atmosphere of the room from start to finish. Make sure you end on a high note so your audience will leave feeling great.

Exercise

Great presenters are always "in the moment," responding to whatever the audience gives them. However, great presenters also come up with solutions/ideas to handle almost any situation they can think of in advance. You're going to have the chance to do that now.

Come up with material for each of the five steps to an effective close that will work for your audience and your presentation.

Step 1: Check that you've addressed any key concerns.

What I plan to do/say/ask:

_____

_____

_____

_____

Step 2: Summarize the benefits of the proposed outcome.

What I plan to do/say/ask:

_____

_____

_____

_____

Step 3: Propose a realistic commitment or advance.

What I plan to do/say/ask:

_____

_____

_____

_____

_____

Step 4: Use a story to close with emotion and achieve your outcome.

What I plan to do/say/ask:

_____

_____

_____

_____

_____

Step 5: Finish at the peak!

What I plan to do/say/ask:

_____

_____

_____

_____

_____

Congratulations! You are now an expert in the FIRE-UP System of powerful presentations. You know how to use the FIRE-UP ladder to create and deliver a talk that will move your audience to action. Now you're ready to take advantage of the expertise of world-class speakers to make your presentations even more powerful and persuasive.

Chapter 15 Highlights

The last step is to propose a commitment and close with connection. There are four possible results you may encounter.

Positive Result #1: Commitment — "Let's do it right now and sign a contract."

Positive Result #2: Advance — they see the value in what you're presenting but they're not quite able to make a commitment. Ask your audience for a small commitment or series of smaller commitments. The key is to be specific.

Negative Result #1: No Agreement — "Thanks, but no thanks." Don't take this response personally, but try to discover the reasons your audience hasn't accepted your solution.

Negative Result #2: Continuation — "Let us think about it and we'll get back to you." The way to deal with continuation is to move your audience to advance (Positive Result #2) by getting a specific commitment.

When challenges or objections come up, you may have talked about the outcome way too early, and/or you haven't created enough pain in your audience's minds. Revisit any of the FIRE-UP steps during your close to reinforce the impact on your audience. There are five steps to help close your audience.
1. Check that you've addressed any key concerns.
2. Summarize the benefits of the proposed outcome.
3. Propose a realistic commitment or advance.
4. Create a lasting connection.
5. Finish at the peak!

Chapter Sixteen
Secrets of the World's Top Speakers

Using the FIRE-UP System, you can be a persuasive presenter and do a great job of getting your point across. But if you're interested in being the absolute best presenter you can be, start by modeling the world's top speakers and presenters. You may have seen some of them: individuals who can hold an audience in the palm of their hands seemingly without effort . . . presenters whose message and delivery touch minds and hearts . . . speakers who seem to be talking directly to every single person in an audience, even if the crowd numbers in the thousands. These people have mastered the ability to connect with their audiences and move them to take action. It's not just what they have to say, it's how they have learned to say it that enables them to have such massive impact. And you can use their secrets to make yourself a more effective presenter as well.

Everything these great presenters do, however, boils down to what I said in Chapter 1: ***Great presentations happen when you allow yourself to create a series of interesting, connected conversations with your audience.*** The secrets in this chapter are merely suggestions that will help your audience feel as if you are speaking to each one of them in turn, and make what you say more interesting by enhancing how you say it.

Secret #1: Communicate with people in all areas of the room.

Have you ever been in the back of a group where the speaker only seems to be talking to the first few rows of people around him or her? Conversely, have you ever been in the front row and felt the speaker was literally talking above your head? Those speakers weren't reaching their entire audience simply because they weren't directing their focus appropriately. Our job as presenters is to make each person in the audience feel as if we are having a connected conversation with him or her. We can do this by focusing our attention in different areas of the room at different times.

I suggest that presenters divide the room into halves, thirds, or sixths (depending on the size of the audience) and then give each section equal attention. When you rehearse your delivery, look at different parts of the room at different times. When I was just starting out as a presenter, I went so far as to mark in my notes "Look left," "Look back," "Look front" to ensure I was covering all areas of the room. If you direct your focus equally throughout the room, most of your audience will feel that you are speaking to them and paying attention to their responses.

Another aspect of communicating equally is to notice if you look toward one side of the audience more than the other. In the same way people are left-handed or right-handed, some speakers tend to look to the right more often than they do to the left, and vice versa. Notice where your attention is going and divide your focus equally between left, center, and right.

Finally, when you focus your attention on a particular section of the room make sure you're really looking at individuals, not just "scanning" the area. I like to say, "When you try to speak to everyone at the same time you end up speaking to no one, but when you speak to one person at a time you end up speaking to everyone." Pick one person and talk directly to him or her for a few seconds, then move on to someone else in the same area. If you are speaking directly to someone, the people around him or her will feel your focus, and it will seem like you are including them in your conversation, too.

Secret #2: Move with purpose.

Movement can be powerful when done with a purpose. As a presenter, the only reason you should move is to create a more powerful connection with somebody. If you've ever seen a presenter or speaker who "wanders"—moving from place to place with no discernible reason other than to move—you know how distracting that can be. However, if you move to make a point or to speak to a different person in the audience, then your movement has a reason and a direction, and it can increase the impact of your presentation.

Depending on the amount of space that you have in the front of the room, you can use movement to help you connect with different people in different parts of the room (see Secret #1). Say you've been focusing on speaking with people in the back left corner of the room for a few minutes. You can choose a person in the front right section, and then move toward the new person while you speak to them. Your movement doesn't have to be huge; taking one step in a different direction will be perceived by your audience as movement, as long as it's done with purpose.

Here are five keys to using movement effectively in your presentations.

1. *Move to a new spot often.* This way you can connect with more people in your audience. Your movement should always be towards the person you are speaking to, and you should keep focused on that person as you move.

2. Once you complete a movement, *stand and deliver from a powerful speaking position.* In observing world-class speakers, I have noticed that they tend to have one foot in front of the other, pointing toward the section of the audience they are speaking to at that moment. If they are speaking to someone on the right side of their audience their right foot will tend to be forward, and if they are speaking to someone on the left side of the audience, their left foot will tend to be forward. Putting one foot slightly ahead of the other points your energy toward the audience. If you're speaking to people in the center, you can choose either foot to have slightly in front of the other. World-

class speakers also tend to lean slightly toward the audience with their weight a little forward. Leaning toward your audience says subliminally that you want to communicate; whenever I see a speaker who is leaning away from the audience, I feel as if the speaker doesn't like the audience or is afraid of them. Your weight ideally should fall about 60 to 80 percent on your front foot and about 20 to 40 percent on your back foot. I call this position—with one foot slightly ahead of the other, weight more on the forward foot—the *Powerful Speaking Position.*

Make sure to avoid any extraneous movement when standing: no swaying, fidgeting, or tapping of feet. When you move, move; when you stand, stand. You can add movement and variety in your standing poses by the use of gestures, voice, and facial expressions (more on these later).

3. *Get close to your audience to create as connected an experience as possible.* Whenever you stand in front of a group of people, there exists a physical as well as mental gap between you as the presenter and them as the audience. To be a truly world-class presenter, you must do everything in your power to eliminate that gap. And one of the best ways to do so is to stand close to your audience.

Both novice and experienced presenters can develop a habit of standing towards the back of the area in which they're presenting. It looks like they're trying to keep as far away from the audience as possible! Physical proximity will help your audience to feel closer to you. When you combine proximity with the forward-leaning stance and movement discussed above, you and your audience will feel a much stronger connection.

4. *Keep your body turned toward your audience as you move.* If at all possible, avoid turning your back on your audience, as this almost always breaks any connection you might have established. Even if you have to move backwards, try to keep part of your body facing your audience. If you're using slides or PowerPoints as part of your presentation, have the projector/laptop controls set up so you can run them while facing your audience.

Another important thing to remember is that when you move and stand on either side of the presentation space, you run the risk of cutting off the people sitting on the other side. Here's what I mean.

When you move to your left and face the people on that side, the members of the audience on the other side (indicated by the shading) will see only your back, unless you make an effort to include them. You can do this by putting your left foot forward and your right foot back, and not turning your body completely to the left but allowing it to face more toward the center.

5. *Create angles with your movement.* Communication is more powerful and charismatic when you move on the diagonal rather than a straight line. It also can create an element of surprise, which will keep your audience interested.

Secret #3: Use your whole body to communicate.

Fifty-five percent of all communication comes through your physiology, so use yours effectively. Use all *three VAK modalities* in your body and voice as well as in your presentation content. If you're talking about how excited the sales staff is going to be with the new equipment you're providing them, you can be in fast, loud visual mode. When you describe all the benefits of the equipment and how it will increase the bottom line, change into auditory (this is the modality where people are best able to absorb factual information). When you tell stories or talk about emotion or how great people will feel, let yourself drop into kinesthetic mode.

If you're a novice presenter, I suggest that you plan in advance certain spots where your content is best delivered in visual, auditory, or kinesthetic mode. After a while using all three modalities in your presentations will become natural.

Here are some specific tips for communicating with your whole body by making the best use of your face, gestures, and posture.

- **Facial expressions.** Start by relaxing your face, and then let it be a mirror of your content. You don't have to work hard on facial expressions, as most people are naturally adept at letting their faces reflect their words.

- **Gestures.** Your hands should be relaxed and out in front of you, and just let them move naturally as you talk. When you're connected emotionally to your content, gestures usually will occur by themselves. If, however, you feel uncomfortable making even the smallest gesture, you might want to practice in front of a mirror until you're confident that you can use your hands to emphasize your words and ideas.

- **Posture.** This is how you hold your body when you're standing still. We talked earlier about foot position, but I want to add one more thing: never stand with your feet together while you're doing a presentation. Standing with your feet together creates a sensation of instability and discomfort in your audience, because it looks like someone could push you over with just a touch. Your feet should be at least hip-width apart. This creates a stable base and a sense of stability and certainty in both you and in your audience. (This is especially key for women, as they often tend to stand with their feet closer together. But ladies, try standing with your feet together, and then stand with your feet about a foot or so apart. You'll feel a greater sense of strength, solidity, and certainty in your body, and those qualities will be communicated to your audience. Most women who do presentations also wear some kind of high heel, and this can cause them to shift their weight backward, off the balls of the feet and onto the heel. But as we said earlier, this creates a sense of distance from your audience. It's important for all presenters to be aware of where their weight is when they are standing, and to lean forward or stand centered rather than leaning back.)

Great presenters are willing to use everything they've got to get their message across to an audience. I've found that the secret to using your whole body isn't planning your gestures in advance, or rehearsing your presentation in front of a mirror. But remember, your primary focus is going to be the content of your presentation, not the delivery. The real secret is to be absolutely committed to connecting with your audience, and be willing to put all of yourself into your presentation during the time you're in front of them. I believe that if you get into the right emotional state and create a series of connected conversations, then the gestures, postures, and facial expressions will occur on their own.

Secret #4: Use your voice to keep them awake and engaged.

What you say is vital, but how you say it makes a huge difference. Thirty-eight percent of your communication comes not from your words but from your voice qualities. There are four vocal qualities that are very easy to change, and they create a lot of vocal interest for your audience: pace, tonality, volume, and pitch.

1. **Pace.** This is the speed at which you talk. Make sure that your regular pace of speech is comfortable for your audience to listen to and understand. You want to make sure you're not talking so fast that no one can understand you, nor so slow that people are falling asleep. However, there are places in each presentation where it's great to talk a little more quickly, and others where you can slow your pace down—to emphasize a point or to tell an emotional story, for example.

2. **Tonality.** Think about the difference between a suggestive voice and a loud, grating shout. That's tonality. Changing your tonality can be very effective in creating interest and conveying meaning. Suppose you wanted to describe an irate customer: changing your tone to be loud, angry, and grating will convey the customer's emotional state instantly. Then, when the company's sales rep handled the customer's problem quickly, you could use a completely different tone to

act out the customer's changed emotional state. Tonal changes are great shorthand for communicating emotion and adding variety to your presentation.

3. **Volume.** You can use loudness, softness or even complete silence to communicate. Make your audience lean in to listen to you, or shake them up a little with a loud, strong declaration. You can use a dramatic pause to get a point across. Just make sure your volume is appropriate to your content: don't shout something that's supposed to be intimate, and don't whisper every time you have an important point to make.

4. **Pitch.** This is a vocal quality that many speakers could use more effectively. For men, using everything from a deep base to a falsetto can be a great asset in making their presentations interesting and their points clear. For women, it's very important that they find a vocal pitch that is in the lower part of their range. High pitches are more difficult for most people to listen to for an extended period of time. That's why women's voices sometimes can be perceived as shrill and grating. Ladies, you don't have to change your voice; just make sure when you're doing a presentation that you start in the lower part of your range, and let yourself go high only for emphasis. Your audience will be more willing to listen to you for longer periods of time.

The key with vocal qualities, as with all the secrets, is to vary them throughout your presentation. Staying in one vocal quality, one modality, or in one place too long will cause your audience to trance out. And you want your audience awake, aware, and interested in what you have to say!

Secret #5: Maintain eye contact with your audience.

A few years ago I decided to try snowboarding. I'd been a skier for a long time, and I thought snowboarding would be easy to pick up—but it wasn't. I fell every time I tried to turn, and I discovered that you hit really hard when you fall because your feet are locked on the board. Luckily, my seven-year-old daughter, Kylie, had been taking snowboarding lessons that day. I asked her what the instructor was teaching them, and she said, "You're supposed to pick out a tree, look at it, shift your weight, and keep going for that tree. You can't look down or you will fall (which is what I was doing); you just look across the other side, pick a tree, shift your weight, and move towards it." I followed Kylie's advice, and by the end of the day I was snowboarding successfully.

The secret to successful snowboarding is the same secret great speakers use in establishing connection with their audience: they shift their eyes and energy from person to person to person. Eye contact is vital for presenters. Your power and your energy go where you look. In order to have a connected conversation, you've got to have enough eye contact for the other person to feel you are truly speaking with them.

A lot of presenters struggle with this concept. Some are afraid of looking at someone for too long. Others are afraid that if they look at someone for five seconds, they're neglecting everyone else. But if you're having a conversation with one person, it's natural to look at them; and it feels much more natural for the rest of the audience as well. Here are some easy ways to establish connection through eye contact.

- **Always look at your audience.** You always want to talk to people, not to floors, ceilings, or carpets. Even as you move, keep your eyes on a member of the audience. Avoid looking down at the ground, over people's heads, at blank spaces, or at the audience as a whole. Even if you're thinking about your content, keep your eyes on the people in your audience.

- **Pick out key people in each section of your audience and stay with each person for at least five seconds.** For people to feel you are really talking to them, you can't just glance their way; you need to focus on them long enough for them to feel you are really with them. I've found that five seconds is the minimum time for most people to feel your focus and attention and respond to it within themselves, setting up the give and take of a connected communication, but you may be with people a little longer or sometimes a little less. The best thing to do is to time your shift from one person to another at points where you are finishing a sentence or a thought.

Secret #6: Have fun!

When you have fun while delivering your presentation, your audience will enjoy it too. If you're worried about your outcome or just plain don't enjoy being in front of people, that worry and discomfort will communicate instantly to your audience. If you've done the physical, mental, and emotional preparation described in Chapters 5 and 6, and if you've put yourself in your OPI, then doing the presentation no matter what the outcome should be an experience you can have fun with. If not, you may want to add "fun" to your OPI emotions!

How to Become a World Class Presenter: Practice!

The only way to get really good at something is to practice. You have a full outline of everything you need to do to be a world-class presenter by using the FIRE-UP System; now it's up to you to use what you know. Especially when you're first starting out, you should set up opportunities to practice everything you've learned in this book.

When I train speakers, I have them start by telling a story that they know. It can be a personal anecdote, a metaphorical story or an account of the last NBA basketball game they watched on TV—content doesn't matter. Each person tells their story in front of a small group of people (usually the other students in the class; if you want to do this on your own, you can have some of your most nonjudgmental friends be your audience). The speakers are allowed to prepare the story the same way they would prepare any presentation. But the goal is to break the ice and get people used to being in front of an audience and using their story to create a series of interesting, connected conversations. (Make sure you tell your audience to applaud madly after you finish!)

The next step is for the speakers to create a four to five-minute presentation and deliver it to the group. This time I ask them to focus a little more on content, creating an outcome and remind the audience of their pain. I ask the audience to pay close attention to each speaker while I take notes on the presentation. (If you're doing this on your own, you may want to have a friend who will take notes for you.) After the speaker is finished everyone applauds, and then we review what the presenter did.

I always start by telling the speaker what they did well—acknowledging people is a key part of developing great speakers. I'll also ask the audience, "What did this person do that made this a great presentation?" Then we'll talk about how the presenter could improve their presentation the next time, eliciting the audience's feedback as well. I specifically ask, "What else could this person have done that would have had an even more powerful impact?"

Finally, we have the presenter do the same speech again, incorporating the feedback he or she has received. This time we use one of the most indispensable tools for coaching presenters: a video camera. There's nothing more informative than seeing yourself on video, watching the ways you successfully communicate with your audience. After the presentation, everyone watches the videotape together, with me, the presenter, and the audience all giving both positive and improvement feedback. This is where we start honing in on the specifics of delivery-movement, varying your voice, eye contact, and so on. Then the presenter gets up immediately and does his or her presentation again, choosing one to three improvements to focus on. This is a great session, as people get a chance to experience how much their presentations change as a result of the feedback. We tape this session, too, and watch the tape together, acknowledging the speaker for all the improvements.

The goal of all these sessions is not just to fix things, but to establish patterns of success for each presenter. Everyone is going to have certain things they do really well, and others they need to work on. By giving people the opportunity to present, get feedback, and then present again while incorporating the suggestions, helps them build the "muscles" that will make them better presenters.

If you are committed to becoming a world-class speaker, practice literally does make perfect. But not just practicing in front of the mirror or a video camera—you must practice in front of other people, to get their immediate responses and to feel the difference between a good presentation and a great one. That's step one. The next step is to do as many presentations as possible. If your job involves doing presentations, great—but there are always opportunities for speakers and presenters. Go to a senior center and talk about one of your hobbies. Ask if you can speak to a class at a local high school or college (educators are always eager for someone with "real life experience" to speak to students). See if you can speak at the local YMCA, political club, or any other group or organization. Just make sure that for every single speech you do, you follow the steps of the FIRE-UP System. Do your preparation. Reinforce your OPI. Set an outcome. Follow every rung of the ladder and deliver your presentation in a series of interesting, connected conversations. When appropriate, ask for feedback at the end of every presentation. People love to be asked their opinion, and they won't hesitate to tell you what they think.

Once you get good at presenting, the key to becoming world-class is to keep stretching. When you first start out, it's important to find your comfort zone so you will seem at ease and natural in front of people. But world-class speakers are always trying new things, seeing how they work, and then trying something else. The great news is that every audience will offer you different challenges and opportunities, so stretching yourself is guaranteed! What will work for one group won't work for another. What works in front of ten people might not work in front of a hundred, or a thousand. With every presentation you need to ask, "How do I stretch myself in order to communicate effectively?" If you are committed to your own growth as well as your audience's, then your presentations will inevitably become better and better.

Ultimately, becoming a world-class speaker really comes down to the heart. World-class speakers care about their audiences, and want to connect with them and to move them to a win/win outcome. They believe in what they have to say and the value of what they have to offer. With love, passion, and belief, they reach both the hearts and minds of their audiences—and enjoy themselves in the process!

Chapter 16 Highlights

Secret #1: Communicate with people in all areas of the room. Divide the room into halves, thirds, or sixths (depending on the size of the audience), and then make sure that they give each section equal attention.

Secret #2: Move with purpose and to a new spot often.
- Once you complete a movement, stand and deliver from a powerful speaking position.
- Get close to your audience to create as connected an experience as possible.
- Always keep your body turned toward your audience as you move.
- Create angles with your movement.

Secret #3: Use your whole body to communicate. Be a VAK-communicate in visual, auditory, and kinesthetic modalities. Use facial expressions, gestures, and posture.

Secret #4: Use your voice to keep your audience awake and engaged. Vary your pace, tonality, volume, and pitch.

Secret #5: Maintain eye contact with your audience. Shift your eyes and energy from person to person. You can maintain eye contact by (1) always looking at your audience instead of the walls, floor, or your PowerPoint; (2) picking out key people in each section of your audience and direct your focus to them periodically, and (3) staying with each person for at least five seconds.

Secret #6: Have fun! When you have fun while delivering your presentation, your audience will enjoy it too. The only way to get really good at something is to practice. Set up opportunities to practice everything you've learned in this book. Establish patterns of success for yourself as a presenter.

Chapter Seventeen
Conclusion:
Climbing the Real Ladder of Success

Let's take a look at our ladder one last time. Hopefully, the ladder, will be a tool you can go to time after time to help you prepare and deliver outstanding presentations.

Focus on Your Outcome!

Propose a commitment and close with emotion

Use their uniqueness to demonstrate a solution

Educate, empower and entertain your audience

Remind your audience of their pain

Inform your audience of your purpose

Focus your audience's attention on you

Preparation

You now have learned a powerful system of presenting which will allow you to be successful in convincing people to adopt the outcome you have chosen. But please remember it's not just achieving success but how you succeed that's truly important. If you're asking people to do something that isn't in their best interests, or if you use underhanded techniques to persuade them, then you're not going to be successful in the long run, mainly because of who you become when you build your life around lies and unethical values.

We've spent a lot of time on the foundation, the goal, and the rungs of the ladder. But if the sides of your ladder—your values—aren't strong, you're not going to achieve any kind of lasting success. Becoming a persuasive presenter is not just about results; it's about how you feel about who you are at the end of the day. If you are presenting with integrity, if the goal of your persuasion is to help your audience achieve an outcome that will benefit them, and if your presentation always stays true to the values you hold most dear, then you will be a success in every single presentation no matter what the result.

Let me close with one of my favorite stories. Once a man and a woman were walking together outside a town. These two people were discontented with their lives. They felt they had so much to offer the world, but they knew they weren't doing so. "If only we could find someone to guide us!" they said. "Someone to show us how to be at our best."

Just then, in the distance they spotted a man in a long cloak. The man appeared to be waving to them, signaling them to come over. As they got closer they saw the man looked very wise. He had a long, white beard and very deep eyes that seemed to look right through them and see their deepest desires.

When the couple reached his side, the man said, "You are in search of something. What is it?"

The couple looked at each other. How could he have known they had just been speaking of that very thing? They replied, "We are looking for someone to show us how to be our best, to help us fulfill our reason for being alive."

"Come with me," the old man said. And he turned and walked into the woods beside the road. The couple was mystified, but they followed.

The old man kept walking through the woods for about five minutes, with the couple following him. Then the woods ended abruptly. The couple stared in shock: they were at the top of a high cliff overlooking a river many hundreds of feet below.

The old man was standing at the very edge of the cliff. He beckoned to them. "Come here," he said.

The couple looked at him in astonishment. "Are you crazy? It's dangerous!" they told him.

"You said you wanted to fulfill your destiny? Then come here," the old man insisted.

"But... we're afraid," the woman said, and her companion added, "If we come too close, we might fall."

"Come to the edge!" the old man said firmly.

The couple looked at each other. Was their destiny worth the risk? Slowly, they approached the old man standing at the edge of the cliff.

"Look out at the horizon," the old man said. The couple turned their backs on the woods and gazed at the sky. All of a sudden they felt a tremendous shove. The old man had pushed them off the cliff!

In that instant . . . they remembered they could fly.

Standing in front of a group of people to persuade them to adopt your outcome can feel like standing at the edge of a cliff. Especially when you first begin presenting, it's natural for fears and doubts to come up. But remember, you too can fly. Sharing your ideas and emotions with people is natural; it's inside you already. If you've ever talked with one other person about something important, you've been a persuasive presenter. Standing in front of a group of people and doing a presentation may feel different, but it's truly not. If you can connect with one other person, then you can use the information in this book to master the art of persuasive presentations.

You have everything you need within you to be a confident, dynamic, ethical, successful, persuasive presenter. It's just a question of whether you are ready to fulfill your destiny and take the leap into the unknown.

Remember—you can fly!

Recommended Resources

8 Keys of Leadership
by Tom McCarthy

For more than a decade, Tom McCarthy, has successfully taught hundreds of thousands of people how to dramatically increase their level of performance in business and personal life. Tom not only speaks about leadership he lives it. **Through these 8 keys Tom will teach you how to improve your Leadership in life.**

- **Formulate**
- **Communicate**
- **Demonstrate**
- **Participate**
- **Delegate**
- **Calibrate**
- **Accelerate**
- **Celebrate**

These **2 audiotapes** were recorded in front of a live audience. The excitement that you hear in these tapes will show you that by using the 8 keys in your life you will have a reason to celebrate.

Perfect for people looking to improve their leadership abilities. Including managers, team leaders, parents and executives.

8 Keys of Leadership audiotape album by Tom McCarthy ISBN 0-9673164-4-8 Item # 316408 $37.00

Order Online at www.TomMcCarthy.com

Step-Up Selling!™
by Tom McCarthy

Very few salespeople truly understand how to persuade ethically and easily. There is however, a research and time-tested pattern of communication that makes selling fun and easy. This program shows you how to mentally prepare yourself, connect with customers, uncover their wants and needs, and then give them what they want with integrity. Whether your just getting started or a seasoned pro, get ready to see your sales soar with 6 audiocassette album and study guide.

The Breakthrough Step-Up System of Selling will help you:

- Increase Your Sales
- Increase Your Level of Customer Satisfaction
- Increase Your Referral Business & Fulfillment as a Salesman
- Increase Your Level of Fulfillment

Perfect for anyone involved in the sales process responsible for selling products or services.

Step-Up Selling!™
by Tom McCarthy
6 Audiocassettes &
Study Guide
ISBN 0-9673164-2-1
Order # 316407
$99.00

Order Online at www.TomMcCarthy.com

FIRE-UP Your Presentations

This is the exact system that Tom has developed over 14 years of giving presentations to consistently perform at his best! In addition to learning the system—you will use it!

You Will Learn:

- How to assess your audience.
- How to define a powerful outcome for each presentation.
- How to organize your thoughts and materials.
- How to create an opening that grabs the audience's attention.
- How to establish a great first impression.
- How to maintain rapport with your audience throughout your presentation.
- How to develop emotional contact with your audience.
- How to influence and teach through telling stories.
- How to make your presentations more lively and interesting.
- How to persuade an audience to action.
- How to communicate competence and confidence.
- How to eliminate emotions that keep you from being your best.
- How to use closings that create a lasting positive impression.

This course is limited to only 17 people so that Tom can provide the maximum hands-on coaching to each participant. You will see a massive improvement in your presentations. Guaranteed. You will have more confidence and actually have fun giving presentations! Plus, you will learn advanced strategies that will allow you to deliver presentations that create lasting impact with your audiences. Are you ready?

*This seminar can also be booked for corporate groups and teams.

Visit www.FireUpPresentations.com for upcoming event dates and locations. Get registered for Tom's Fire-Up System today!

Finally, a speaker that delivers more than what is expected!

Finding a speaker is easy, but it is difficult to find someone who makes an immediate impact on your audience and creates long-term results. Especially, someone who matches your outcome with the appropriate message and exercises to take your organization to even higher levels of performance. Bold claim . . . you bet—and we guarantee it!

Now, the real truth about peak performance . . .

Face it, people are creatures of habit. So you can waste valuable resources bringing in a "motivational" speaker who may entertain, amuse and teach a few skills, but just having new information isn't enough to make lasting changes. In order to reach higher levels of peak performance people have to be challenged. During our programs you experience the skills using cutting-edge techniques in inspiring and practical ways. Your audience will leave with the new skills, and with the inspiration to manifest enhanced performance on a regular basis.

Programs Available:

- **Breakthrough to Greatness.** How to create a culture that creates individual and organizational breakthroughs.
- **FIRE-UP Your Presentations.** How to design and deliver presentations that get outstanding results.
- **STEP-UP Your Sales.** A proven selling system that closes more sales and significantly increases.
- **TRUE Leadership.** How to create and empower outstanding teams.

**Visit www.TomMcCarthy.com
to book Tom for your next event or seminar!**

ORDER FORM

Tom McCarthy's Recommended Resources	Price	Qty	Total
Step-Up Selling™ by Tom McCarthy 6 Audiocassettes & Study Guide Order # 316407	$99		
8 Keys of Leadership Audiotape album by Tom McCarthy Order # 316408	$37		

United Parcel Shipping Table

Order Total	2-Day	Ground
$50.00 or under	$11.60	$5.50
$50.01-$250.00	$13.20	$6.00
$250.01-$over	$16.20	$7.50

Subtotal $ _____

For Alaska, Hawaii, and Canada, figure the total of your order, plus the regular shipping cost, and add 10%. For foreign and overseas orders, figure the total of your order, plus the regular shipping cost, and add 20%.

Shipping (see chart) $ _____

Terms: 60-day money back guarantee! Contact us within 60 days of your invoice date if, for any reason, you're not 100% satisfied with any product you've received from us. Product must be in resaleable condition.
Customer Service: 1-800-946-7804 or (316) 942-1111

TOTAL $ _____

PAYMENT TYPE: Visa   MC   AMEX   Discover   or   Check   Cash

Please print clearly

Credit Card # _ _ _ _ _ _ _ _ _ _ _ _ _ _ _ _

Expires: (MM/YY) _____ / _____   Signature: _____

Full Name:

Address:
Apt./Suite#

City: **State:**   **Zip:**   **Country:**

Phone: **Email:**

www.TomMcCarthy.com
Tom McCarthy Enterprises, Inc.
P.O. Box 132
Rancho Santa Fe, CA 92067 USA
Tel: (858) 759-8484